FREE Test Taking Tips DVD Offer

To help us better serve you, we have developed a Test Taking Tips DVD that we would like to give you for <u>FREE</u>. **This DVD covers world-class test taking tips that you can use to be even more successful when you are taking your test.**

All that we ask is that you email us your feedback about your study guide. Please let us know what you thought about it – whether that is good, bad or indifferent.

To get your **FREE Test Taking Tips DVD**, email <u>freedvd@studyguideteam.com</u> with "FREE Test Taking Tips DVD" in the subject line and the following information in the body of the email:

    a. The title of your study guide.

    b. Your product rating on a scale of 1-5, with 5 being the highest rating.

    c. Your feedback about the study guide. What did you think of it?

    d. Your full name and shipping address to send your free DVD.

If you have any questions or concerns, please don't hesitate to contact us at <u>freedvd@studyguideteam.com</u>.

Thanks again!

ACSM Personal Trainer Certification Review Study Guide

Table of Contents

Quick Overview

As you draw closer to taking your exam, preparing becomes more and more important. Thankfully, you have this study guide to help you get ready. Use this guide to help keep your studying on track and refer to it often.

This study guide contains several key sections that will help you be successful on your exam. The guide contains tips for what you should do the night before and the day of the test. Also included are test-taking tips. Knowing the right information is not always enough. Many well-prepared test takers struggle with exams. These tips will help equip you to accurately read, assess, and answer test questions.

A large part of the guide is devoted to showing you what content to expect on the exam and to helping you better understand that content. Near the end of this guide is a practice test so that you can see how well you have grasped the content. Then, answers explanations are provided so that you can understand why you missed certain questions.

Don't try to cram the night before you take your exam. This is not a wise strategy for a few reasons. First, your retention of the information will be low. Your time would be better used by reviewing information you already know rather than trying to learn lots of new information. Second, you will likely become stressed as you try to gain large amount of knowledge in a short amount of time. Third, you will be depriving yourself of sleep. So be sure to go to bed at a reasonable time the night before. Being well-rested helps you focus and remain calm.

Be sure to eat a substantial breakfast the morning of the exam. If you are taking the exam in the afternoon, be sure to have a good lunch as well. Being hungry is distracting and can make it difficult to focus. You have hopefully spent lots of time preparing for the exam. Don't let an empty stomach get in the way of success!

When travelling to the testing center, leave earlier than needed. That way, you have a buffer in case you experience any delays. This will help you remain calm and will keep you from missing your appointment time at the testing center.

Be sure to pace yourself during the exam. Don't try to rush through the exam. There is no need to risk performing poorly on the exam just so you can leave the testing center early. Allow yourself to use all of the allotted time if needed.

Remain positive while taking the exam even if you feel like you are performing poorly. Thinking about the content you should have mastered will not help you perform better on the exam.

Once the exam is complete, take some time to relax. Even if you feel that you need to take the exam again, you will be well served by some down time before you begin studying again. It's often easier to convince yourself to study if you know that it will come with a reward!

Test-Taking Strategies

1. Predicting the Answer

When you feel confident in your preparation for a multiple-choice test, try predicting the answer before reading the answer choices. This is especially useful on questions that test objective factual knowledge or that ask you to fill in a blank. By predicting the answer before reading the available choices, you eliminate the possibility that you will be distracted or led astray by an incorrect answer choice. You will feel much more confident in your selection if you read the question, predict the answer, and then find your prediction among the answer choices. After using this strategy, be sure to still read all of the answer choices carefully and completely. If you feel unprepared, you should not attempt to predict the answers. This would be a waste of time and an opportunity for your mind to wander in the wrong direction.

2. Reading the Whole Question

Too often, test takers scan a multiple-choice question, recognize a few familiar words, and immediately jump to the answer choices. Test authors are aware of this common impatience, and they will sometimes prey upon it. For instance, a test author might subtly turn the question into a negative, or he or she might redirect the focus of the question right at the end. The only way to avoid falling into these traps is to read the entirety of the question carefully before reading the answer choices.

3. Looking for Wrong Answers

Long and complicated multiple-choice questions can be intimidating. One way to simplify a difficult multiple-choice question is to eliminate all of the answer choices that are clearly wrong. In most sets of answers, there will be at least one selection that can be dismissed right away. If the test is administered on paper, the test taker could draw a line through it to indicate that it may be ignored; otherwise, the test taker will have to perform this operation mentally or on scratch paper. In either case, once the obviously incorrect answers have been eliminated, the remaining choices may be considered. Sometimes identifying the clearly wrong answers will give the test taker some information about the correct answer. For instance, if one of the remaining answer choices is a direct opposite of one of the eliminated answer choices, it may well be the correct answer. The opposite of obviously wrong is obviously right! Of course, this is not always the case. Some answers are obviously incorrect simply because they are irrelevant to the question being asked. Still, identifying and eliminating some incorrect answer choices is a good way to simplify a multiple-choice question.

4. Don't Overanalyze

Anxious test takers often overanalyze questions. When you are nervous, your brain will often run wild causing you to make associations and discover clues that don't actually exist. If you feel that this may be a problem for you, do whatever you can to slow down during the test. Try taking a deep breath or counting to ten. As you read and consider the question, restrict yourself to the particular words used by the author. Avoid thought tangents about what the author *really* meant, or what he or she was *trying* to say. The only things that matter on a multiple-choice test are the words that are actually in the question. You must avoid reading too much into a multiple-choice question, or supposing that the writer meant something other than what he or she wrote.

5. No Need for Panic

It is wise to learn as many strategies as possible before taking a multiple-choice test, but it is likely that you will come across a few questions for which you simply don't know the answer. In this situation, avoid panicking. Because most multiple-choice tests include dozens of questions, the relative value of a single wrong answer is small. Moreover, your failure on one question has no effect on your success elsewhere on the test. As much as possible, you should compartmentalize each question on a multiple-choice test. In other words, you should not allow your feelings about one question to affect your success on the others. When you find a question that you either don't understand or don't know how to answer, just take a deep breath and do your best. Read the entire question slowly and carefully. Try rephrasing the question a couple of different ways. Then, read all of the answer choices carefully. After eliminating obviously wrong answers, make a selection and move on to the next question.

6. Confusing Answer Choices

When working on a difficult multiple-choice question, there may be a tendency to focus on the answer choices that are the easiest to understand. Many people, whether consciously or not, gravitate to the answer choices that require the least concentration, knowledge, and memory. This is a mistake. When you come across an answer choice that is confusing, you need to give it extra attention. A question might be confusing because you do not know the subject matter to which it refers. If this is the case, don't eliminate the answer before you have affirmatively settled on another. When you come across an answer choice of this type, set it aside as you look at the remaining choices. If you can confidently assert that one of the other choices is correct, you can leave the confusing answer aside. Otherwise, you will need to take a moment to try to better understand the confusing answer choice. Rephrasing is one way to tease out the sense of a confusing answer choice.

7. Your First Instinct

Many people struggle with multiple-choice tests because they overthink the questions. If you have studied sufficiently for the test, you should be prepared to trust your first instinct once you have carefully and completely read the question and all of the answer choices. There is a great deal of research to suggest that the mind can come to the correct conclusion very quickly once it has obtained all of the relevant information. At times, it may seem to you as if your intuition is working faster even than your reasoning mind. This may in fact be true. The knowledge you obtain while studying may be retrieved from your subconscious before you have a chance to work out the associations that support it. Verify your instinct by working out the reasons that it should be trusted.

8. Key Words

Many test takers struggle with multiple-choice questions because they have poor reading comprehension skills. Quickly reading and understanding a multiple-choice question requires a mixture of skill and experience. To help with this, try jotting down a few key words and phrases on a piece of scrap paper. Doing this concentrates the process of reading and forces the mind to weigh the relative importance of the question's parts. In selecting words and phrases to write down, the test taker thinks about the question more deeply and carefully. This is especially true for multiple-choice questions that are preceded by a long prompt.

9. Subtle Negatives

One of the oldest tricks in the multiple-choice test writer's book is to subtly reverse the meaning of a question with a word like *not* or *except*. If you are not paying attention to each word in the question, you can easily be led astray by this trick. For instance, a common question format is, "Which of the following is…?" Obviously, if the question instead is, "Which of the following is not….?," then the answer will be quite different. Even worse, the test makers are aware of the potential for this mistake and will include one answer choice that would be correct if the question were not negated or reversed. A test taker who misses the reversal will find what he or she believes to be a correct answer and will be so confident that he or she will fail to reread the question and discover the original error. The only way to avoid this is to practice a wide variety of multiple-choice questions and to pay close attention to each and every word.

10. Reading Every Answer Choice

It may seem obvious, but you should always read every one of the answer choices! Too many test takers fall into the habit of scanning the question and assuming that they understand the question because they recognize a few key words. From there, they pick the first answer choice that answers the question they believe they have read. Test takers who read all of the answer choices might discover that one of the latter answer choices is actually *more* correct. Moreover, reading all of the answer choices can remind you of facts related to the question that can help you arrive at the correct answer. Sometimes, a misstatement or incorrect detail in one of the latter answer choices will trigger your memory of the subject and will enable you to find the right answer. Failing to read all of the answer choices is like not reading all of the items on a restaurant menu. You might miss out on the perfect choice.

11. Spot the Hedges

One of the keys to success on multiple-choice tests is paying close attention to every word. This is never more true than with words like *almost, most, some,* and *sometimes.* These words are called "hedges", because they indicate that a statement is not totally true or not true in every place and time. An absolute statement will contain no hedges, but in many subjects, like literature and history, the answers are not always straightforward. There are always exceptions to the rules in these subjects. For this reason, you should favor those multiple-choice questions that contain hedging language. The presence of qualifying words indicates that the author is taking special care with his or her words, which is certainly important when composing the right answer. After all, there are many ways to be wrong, but there is only one way to be right! For this reason, it is wise when taking a multiple-choice test to avoid answers that are absolute. An absolute answer is one that says things are either all one way or all another. They often include words like *every, always, best,* and *never.* If you are taking a multiple-choice test in a subject that doesn't lend itself to absolute answers, be on your guard if you see any of these words.

12. Long Answers

In many subject areas, the answers are not simple. As already mentioned, the right answer often requires hedges. Another common feature of the answers to a complex or subjective question are qualifying clauses, which are groups of words that subtly modify the meaning of the sentence. If the question or answer choice describes a rule to which there are exceptions or the subject matter is complicated, ambiguous, or confusing, the correct answer will require many words in order to be expressed clearly and accurately. In essence, you should not be deterred by answer choices that seem excessively long. Oftentimes, the author of the text will not be able to write the correct answer without offering some qualifications and modifications. As a test taker, your job is to read the answer choices thoroughly and completely and to select the one that most accurately and precisely answers the question.

13. Restating to Understand

Sometimes, a question on a multiple-choice test is difficult not because of what it asks but because of how it is written. If this is the case, restate the question or answer choice in different words. This process serves a couple of important purposes. First, it forces you to concentrate on the core of the question. In order to rephrase the question accurately, you have to understand it well. Rephrasing the question will concentrate your mind on the key words and ideas. Second, it will present the information to your mind in a fresh way. This process may trigger your memory of some useful scrap of information picked up while studying.

14. True Statements

Sometimes an answer choice will be true in itself, but it does not answer the question. This is one of the main reasons why it is essential to read the question carefully and completely before proceeding to the answer choices. Too often, test takers skip ahead to the answer choices and look for true statements. Having found one of these, they are content to select it without reference to the question above. Obviously, this provides an easy way for test makers to play tricks. The savvy test taker will always read the entire question before turning to the answer choices. Then, having settled on a correct answer choice, he or she will refer to the original question and ensure that the selected answer is relevant. The mistake of choosing a correct-but-irrelevant answer choice is especially common on questions related to specific pieces of objective knowledge, like historical or scientific facts. A prepared test taker will have a wealth of factual knowledge at his or her disposal, but may be careless in its application.

15. No Patterns

One of the more dangerous ideas that circulate about multiple-choice tests is that the correct answers tend to fall into patterns. These erroneous ideas range from a belief that B and C are the most common right answers, to the idea that an unprepared test-taker should answer "A-B-A-C-A-D-A-B-A." It cannot be emphasized enough that pattern-seeking of this type is exactly the WRONG way to approach a multiple-choice test. To begin with, it is highly unlikely that the test maker will plot the correct answers according to some predetermined pattern. The questions are scrambled and delivered in a random order. Furthermore, even if the test maker was following a pattern in the assignation of correct answers, there is no reason why the test maker would know which pattern he or she was using. Any attempt to discern a pattern in the answer choices is a waste of time and a distraction from the real work of taking the test. A test taker would be much better served by extra preparation before the test than by reliance on a pattern in the answers.

Initial Client Consultation and Assessment

Preparation for initial potential client visit

When preparing for an initial client consultation, the personal trainer should have the following items prepared for discussion: necessary documents for the client, expectations for the client, expectations of the personal trainer, accurate pricing for sessions, payment expectations (i.e., when payment is due, and what forms of payment are accepted), and on what terms a client is expected to give notice prior to missing a planned session. For instance, the personal trainer should clearly discuss how soon notice must be given prior to a session being missed before the session fee is forfeited by the client. The trainer must also be prepared to give the client a tour of the fitness facilities and explain whether any equipment is necessary for purchase prior to meeting for the first training session (i.e., proper exercise clothing and footwear, etc.). The client should clearly understand what will happen at the first session and when the paperwork is due, especially if medical clearance is necessary.

Paperwork

The personal trainer must have the client fill out the following paperwork: Health History Questionnaire, Par-Q & You, and a Client Participation Contract. The personal trainer must decide if any other contracts or agreements need to be signed, for instance, a payment agreement form, medical clearance form, etc. All paperwork must be completed prior to exercise testing. If the Par-Q & You and/or the Health History Questionnaire indicate medical clearance is required prior to exercise participation, the trainer must clearly explain this to the client and have the client obtain clearance with a medical clearance form. It is also a professional obligation to let any medical staff intimately involved with a client's ongoing care know about exercise plans.

Effectively communicating expectations

At the initial client session, the personal trainer must clearly communicate future expectations for the client. Some expectations can include the following: timeliness, dress, and level of exertion/discomfort to be expected. Expectations should be shared in an encouraging way and with positive nonverbal communication, for instance, eye contact, firm but kind tone of voice, smile, etc. The personal trainer should provide an explanation of how goals will be created and assessed in an ongoing fashion. Time should be given for the client to ask questions; the client should always feel free to ask questions at any time and participate in future goal setting.

Proper communication

The personal trainer can communicate through various means with the client. Communication should be maintained on a professional level, yet remain friendly and encouraging towards the client. Communication can take place in the following ways: verbally (verbal instruction), nonverbally (eye contact, tone of voice, gestures), written (newsletters, handouts, articles, brochures), email (updates on progress, session reminders), phone, or text messaging. In communicating with a client, the personal trainer needs to keep in mind principles of confidentiality and share client information only with those for whom written consent has been obtained. Text messaging and phone calls from the trainer's personal phone should be used with care and only when other means of communication are unavailable in order to keep a professional relationship with the client.

Prescreening clients prior to exercise instruction

It is important to prescreen clients in order to assess their medical risk. Once medical risk is assessed, appropriate goals and exercise sessions can be planned. Understanding the client's medical risk factors also helps the personal trainer to know whether medical consent must be given in order to begin training. The most common forms for personal trainer use include the following: health/medical history questionnaire, informed consent, trainer-client contract, and policies/procedures.

- Health/medical history questionnaire: Par-Q & You or general health questionnaire that assesses common risk factors related to exercise and indicates whether medical clearance must be given.
- Informed consent: ensures the client understands the relative risks and discomforts associated with exercise sessions.
- Trainer-client contract: the agreed-upon sessions and pricing, signed by both the trainer and the client.
- Policies/procedures: the agreed-upon procedures and policies necessary to provide a positive experience for clients and ensure their goals are met; can include guidelines for missed sessions, appropriate dress, etc.

Medical clearance

According to the Par-Q & You form, medical clearance is necessary for client participation in an exercise program when one or more questions have been answered with a "yes," the client is over 40, and has been inactive for a substantial period of time. On other health history questionnaires, any condition that is not currently under observation by medical personnel must be noted and recommended to a physician's attention. Depending on the conditions present in the client, written permission from the physician may be all that is necessary; however, certain cardiovascular issues may need to be assessed through a physician-handled stress test. Medical clearance must be obtained prior to the initial exercise testing; however, a client may not have any negative health indicators based on completion of the initial paperwork. A medical issue may arise during the initial exercise testing or in subsequent sessions. If this is the case, medical clearance should be recommended and obtained immediately.

Use of screening information to develop overall goals

Initial screening information includes information gathered from both the paperwork and fitness testing of the client. From the paperwork, the personal trainer understands what are the client's personal goals, level of motivation, and health challenges. From the fitness testing, the personal trainer evaluates physiological deficiencies in the client's training. The client then develops goals with the following criteria in mind: begin with the greatest deficiencies and work down to the lesser ones, connect each specific goal with an area of weakness and clearly show how the goal will strengthen it, make the goal measureable and attainable. Creating a measurable and attainable goal also requires creating a rubric which will assess the client progress at regular intervals.

Overview of fitness facility and equipment

It is up to the personal trainer to ensure that the client understands how to properly use equipment in the training facility. This can be done in a variety of ways. The trainer must make sure the client understands the location of everything in the fitness center (i.e., locker rooms, bathrooms, equipment rooms, towels, etc.). The trainer must also ensure in an ongoing fashion that the client knows what is expected at each exercise session. This can be done through providing verbal and nonverbal cues, demonstrating the movement, etc. Give the client time to ask questions about equipment usage, especially if it is expected that the client come to the fitness center at times other than the scheduled sessions.

Dangers of beginning a training regimen without proper paperwork on file

It is never advisable to begin training a client without all of the paperwork in order and signatures in place. If an adequate health history is not present, the trainer will not know if the client is susceptible to certain cardiovascular disease that could cause complications during training sessions. If medical clearance is not obtained when it should be, the personal trainer could be held liable for anything that may happen to the client during an exercise session. If an informed consent is not obtained, the client can hold the trainer liable for any discomforts felt to be out of the ordinary during an exercise session. Although not as serious as the previously mentioned paperwork, if there are no policies or procedures clearly outlined, both the trainer and the client can experience a very dissatisfying professional relationship because neither one knows what to expect from the other at each session. Finally, if there is an absence of paperwork, the trainer is unable to create and communicate effective goals for the client.

Familiarity with ACSM risk factors

The personal trainer should be familiar with ACSM risk factors for cardiovascular, pulmonary, and metabolic diseases prior to meeting with a client for paperwork review because it is necessary for analyzing the completed paperwork. If the trainer is unable to stratify the client's risk, the goal-setting process will lack true substance. Additionally, the trainer will be unable to identify whether the client needs additional medical clearance in order to participate in an exercise program. It is further helpful to be well-versed with the various risk factors so that symptoms noted during exercise that might be detrimental can be evaluated and modifications made.

Possible symptoms of disease

Chronic cardiovascular disease
Clients should be observed for symptoms of coronary artery disease as well as cardiovascular disease, as both can be common. The following symptoms can be observed in clients who may be at a higher risk for coronary artery disease: high blood pressure (at least 140/90 or above; it is best to measure it at two different sessions for accuracy), high cholesterol (HDL of <40 mg/dl, LDL of >130 mg/dl, high triglycerides), uncontrolled high blood sugar (fasting blood glucose level of >60 mg/dl), obesity (BMI of 30 kg/m^2 or higher), sedentary lifestyle (exercises rarely to never), history of smoking or currently smoking, and family history of heart attack or coronary revascularization or sudden death (in a male age 55 or under who is a father or immediate relative, in a female age 65 or under who is a mother or immediate relative). These risk factors are clearly indicated on the Health History Questionnaire for the personal trainer to observe. The following symptoms can be observed in clients who may be at risk for cardiovascular disease: a lack of adequate circulation which can lead to pain or discomfort in the arms, chest, neck, or jaw; experiencing shortness of breath even though not expending a high amount of energy or effort; dizziness or fainting spells; experiencing discomfort during breathing when lying down or at night; swelling of the ankles; heart palpitations (abnormal heart beat) or tachycardia (rapid heartbeat); cramping and sensations of weakness in the legs when walking; heart murmur; unusual levels of fatigue.

Chronic pulmonary disease
The symptoms indicating pulmonary disease are similar to those indicating cardiovascular disease and are as follows: a lack of adequate circulation which can lead to pain or discomfort in the arms, chest, neck, or jaw; experiencing shortness of breath even though not expending a high amount of energy or effort; dizziness or fainting (syncope) spells; experiencing discomfort during breathing when lying down (orthopnea) or at night (nocturnal dyspnea); swelling (edema) of the ankles; heart palpitations (abnormal heartbeat) or tachycardia (rapid heartbeat); cramping and sensations of weakness in the legs when walking; heart murmur; unusual levels of fatigue. Since indications are similar between the two conditions, it is of paramount importance to be in close contact with medical personnel to relay your observations.

Chronic metabolic disease

The following symptoms may indicate that a client has metabolic disease: excess abdominal fat (women: waist circumference > 88cm, men: waist circumference > 102cm), high triglyceride levels (> 150mg/dl), low HDL cholesterol (< 40mg/dl), high fasting glucose levels (> 110mg/dl), and high blood pressure (> 130/85 mmHg). Types of metabolic disease have traditionally included Type 1 and 2 Diabetes, although any disease that interferes with the metabolic processing of nutrients that enter the body is considered metabolic disease. Diseases such as polycystic ovarian syndrome, dementia, cancer, and fatty liver (not due to excess alcohol consumption) are also included in this list.

ACSM model for risk stratification

The ACSM model for risk stratification identifies several different areas for the personal trainer to assess. When assessing risk factors, the personal trainer makes a list of the positive and negative risk factors. Next, the client can be placed in either a low-, moderate-, or high-risk stratum. To be considered in the low-risk stratum, the client must be younger, asymptomatic, or meet only one of the risk factors for cardiovascular or pulmonary disease. To be considered in the moderate-risk stratum, the client must be older (men aged $\geq$45, women aged $\geq$55) and meet the lower threshold of no more than two of the risk factors for cardiovascular or pulmonary disease. To be considered in the high-risk stratum, the client must have known disease (cardiovascular, pulmonary, or metabolic) or have one of the risk factors indicating cardiovascular or pulmonary disease. Clients who are moderate risk and high risk should be supervised by a physician prior to maximal exercise testing. Clients at low and moderate risk may safely engage in submaximal exercise testing.

It is imperative for the personal trainer to know the ACSM guidelines for risk stratification and be able to utilize them on a regular basis. The personal trainer must also understand that assessment is an ongoing process. Understanding and using the ACSM guidelines to stratify client risk allows the trainer to minimize liability in case the client has complications during any of the exercise sessions. It also allows the trainer to more accurately create goals and proper exercise prescriptions to minimize client symptoms.

Plan of action if symptoms of disease are observed

If the client has completed the initial paperwork and a chronic cardiovascular, pulmonary, or metabolic tendency is observed, the personal trainer must clearly communicate the findings with the client and indicate why disease might be indicated. The personal trainer must then recommend that the client seek medical attention and receive medical permission to exercise prior to beginning sessions. If the client is already under medical supervision, it is appropriate for the personal trainer to call the primary physician to discuss the plans for client fitness. It is best to receive medical permission for exercise in writing from the doctor so the trainer can decrease personal liability.

Creating an exercise program

The personal trainer must take all initial paperwork and the initial exercise testing and observe the following: health risks; lifestyle behaviors; basic nutritional habits; positive behaviors; personal goals; baseline levels of muscular endurance, strength, and power; flexibility; and level of cardiovascular fitness. Next, the trainer should create a list of goals according to the greatest deficiencies in the client's lifestyle and fitness level. The trainer needs to be sure to include issues that the client desires to improve as well. Each session that is designed should meet one or more of the goals at a time, with the amount of time allotted to each goal directly proportional to the greatest area of deficiency.

Communication with medical personnel

If it is deemed necessary for the client to seek medical care due to the results from the health history questionnaire, or if the client is already under care of a physician and still shows significant risk after the risk stratification process, it is up to the personal trainer to contact the physician via phone or in person. The trainer must be prepared to discuss exercise plans with the physician and needs to consider when it would be necessary to give updates on client progress to the physician. Depending on the physician's desired level of involvement, the personal trainer must be prepared to give detailed written, electronic, or verbal communication about the client's fitness progress.

Health behavior change models

The client can experience lasting change when he has the support of people around him, for instance, family and friends. The personal trainer must help the client understand how to troubleshoot and identify ways he sabotages his own ability to change. It is important to provide ways to combat this sabotage so the client can have the best chance of maintaining his goals. Health behavior change models can be helpful for the personal trainer to know so that she can utilize this information to reinforce positive behaviors. Some examples of health behavior change models are as follows:

- The socio-ecologic model: This model helps the trainer understand the different variables affecting her client's motivation to move. Often the client has been motivated by national trends or news, or community/organizational/family relationships. These areas can either positively or negatively affect the client's continuing change.
- Readiness to change model: The client has passed through one or more of the stages of change—pre-contemplation, contemplation, preparation, action, motivation. Identifying where he is on the continuum helps the trainer apply proper motivational technique.
- Social cognitive theory: The theory asserts that learning occurs in a social context with observation being the primary means of learning.
- Theory of planned behavior: Three different types of beliefs—behavioral, normative, and control beliefs—motivate behavior.

Goal setting

The purpose of goal setting for clients is twofold: the client needs to understand his initial evaluation in light of where he should be with his health and needs to understand how to achieve optimal health by crossing that gap. With such an important role to fill, goals need to be simple, measurable, achievable, and realistic. Each exercise session should clearly align with a goal. In order to remain simple, there should be one goal for each area of fitness (cardiovascular, muscular strength/power/endurance, and flexibility). Depending on how many sessions the client has contracted, the trainer can decide how many times the goals will be assessed. This needs to be done at regular intervals so the client sees progress clearly. Goals will set the tone and provide purpose for the workouts. This needs to be clearly communicated to the client so he can see how each individual session is important to the overall picture of his health.

Realistic goals to reinforce positive behavior change
When goals are realistic, the client achieves them in a timely manner. When a client sees that she is achieving goals and making gains in her health, she is more likely to continue in the positive changes being made. A realistic goal allows the client to begin with something she feels confident about changing, which leads her to be motivated to change things she thought would be too difficult.

Social support

Social support from organizations, family, and friends can greatly hinder or help a client change negative behaviors into positive ones. For instance, a client's workplace or health insurance may offer incentives that reward becoming part of a fitness center, exercising regularly, or getting nutritional counseling. Family and friends can provide emotional support that helps motivate a client to move past the discomfort of fitness to really achieve results. An unhealthy work environment or negative feedback from family and friends can discourage a client from maintaining new positive habits. In this case, the personal trainer needs to provide the motivation and encouragement that will not be found in other places.

Goals for five areas of fitness

Cardiovascular fitness: The client will be able to run 1 mile without stopping to walk within the next 3 weeks.

Muscular strength: The client will be able hold the plank position for 1 full minute within the next 2 weeks.

Muscular endurance: The client will be able to perform 50 curl-ups in 1 minute within the next 3 weeks.

Muscular power: The client will be able to complete 3 sets of jump squats, single leg hops, and hurdles in 20 minutes within the next month.

Flexibility: The client will be able touch the floor in the double leg hamstring stretch within the next month.

Body fat assessment: The client will reduce total body fat by 2% within the next month.

Structure of bones, skeletal muscle, and connective tissue

Most of the bones of the appendicular skeleton have an epiphysis (head) and a diaphysis (shaft). There is also an outer layer of the bone (periosteum) and an inner layer of the bone (endosteum). Spongy bone can be found inside the epiphysis of the bone and contains blood vessels. Articular cartilage can be found outside the epiphysis at the connecting site of a joint. Skeletal muscle is striated with multiple nuclei. It most often has bony attachments and is voluntary. There are three types of connective tissue: loose (includes areolar, adipose, and reticular), dense (includes dense regular and dense irregular), and cartilage (hyaline, elastic, and fibrocartilage).

Connective tissue

Connective tissue connects muscles and/or bones together throughout the body. Tendons connect muscle to bone, and ligaments connect bone to bone. Both tendons and ligaments (dense regular connective tissue) serve a protective function by holding muscles and bones in their proper place and aiding in proper range of motion. When tendons and ligaments are stretched beyond their capacity, an injury can occur. The personal trainer must understand that working muscles and their corresponding joints outside of their normal range of motion can cause excess stretching in the ligaments and possible damage. In addition, overuse injuries and excessive repetitive force can cause tendon damage. The trainer must be aware of preexisting weaknesses in connective tissue before proceeding to a training program with a client. Loose connective tissue can be found around the organs (areolar), under the skin (adipose), and in bone marrow (reticular). Cartilage can be found in the ribs/nose/trachea/larynx (hyaline), external ear (elastic), and in vertebral discs and knees (fibrocartilage).

Anatomy of cardiovascular and respiratory systems

The basic anatomy of the cardiovascular system is as follows: heart (right and left atrium, right and left ventricle, bicuspid valve, tricuspid valve, pulmonary semilunar valve, aortic semilunar valve, aorta, superior and inferior vena cava) and blood vessels (arteries, arterioles, veins, venules, capillaries). The basic anatomy of the respiratory system is as follows: nose, sinuses, pharynx, larynx, trachea, bronchi, bronchioles, alveoli. Blood that is deoxygenated flows through the superior and inferior vena cava into the right atrium. The right atrium contracts, pushing blood through the tricuspid valve and into the right ventricle. The right ventricle then contracts, the tricuspid valve closes, and the blood is forced through the pulmonary semilunar valve. The pulmonary arteries carry the blood into the alveolar capillaries where oxygen is absorbed and carbon dioxide is removed. The pulmonary veins carry blood back to the left atrium. The left atrium contracts and the blood moves into the left ventricle through the bicuspid valve. The left ventricle contracts and the bicuspid valve closes; blood then is forced into the aortic valve where it goes into coronary and systemic circulation.

Heart rate and blood pressure during exercise

During exercise, heart rate increases linearly along with the increase in intensity. Heart rate is also affected by age, body position (sitting, standing, lying), fitness ability, activity type, presence of heart disease, medications, blood volume, and environmental factors (heat, humidity, cold). Systolic blood pressure behaves in a similar manner and also increases linearly with the exercise workload. Diastolic blood pressure may decrease slightly or remain unchanged throughout the duration because there is a decrease in peripheral resistance so that the working muscles may receive the blood, and thus oxygen, that they need.

Effect of breathing on exercise

Since breathing allows the body to absorb oxygen through the alveoli and clear the carbon dioxide from the system, it is important that the client not hyperventilate (breathe too quickly) during the exercise session. When this happens, there is not sufficient time to clear the carbon dioxide from the body during respiratory processes, and fatigue quickly ensues, leading to a premature ending of the exercise session. The Valsalva maneuver (holding one's breath while straining) is also detrimental to exercise because holding one's breath causes an unnatural rise in heart rate and blood pressure and can lead to extreme discomfort, fainting, or dizziness. It is the personal trainer's job to remind the client to breathe at the appropriate times.

Directions of body movement

The directions of the body are as follows: inferior (toward the feet), superior (toward the head), medial (toward the midline of the body), lateral (away from the midline of the body), pronation (rolling inward), supination (rolling outward), flexion (movement that decreases the joint angle), extension (movement that increases the joint angle), hyperextension (movement that increases the joint angle unnaturally), adduction (movement toward the midline of the body), abduction (movement away from the midline of the body), rotation (movement to the right or left, usually of the head and neck), circumduction (compound circular movement including flexion, extension, abduction, adduction), agonist (initiates movement), antagonist (opposes the agonist muscle action), stabilizer (contracts to hold one body part immobile so another body part can be mobile).

Relation of directions and planes of movement to resistance exercise

Understanding the directions to describe exercises is essential to putting together a well-rounded exercise routine. It also allows the personal trainer to assess full range of motion for joints and give proper instruction to the client during each session. The trainer is provided a limitless array of modifications and ways to make the workout more challenging for the client as needed simply by changing the direction of the movement. It also allows the trainer to observe abnormal patterns of movement that exist in the client and that can be fixed.

Planes of movement

The planes of movement are as follows: frontal/coronal (divides the body into front and back sections), sagittal (divides the body into right and left sections), midsagittal (divides the body into equal right and left sections), transverse (divides the body into top and bottom sections). Understanding the different planes of movement allows the personal trainer to effectively create exercise routines that work each section of the body independently or in conjunction with the others. It allows weaker muscle groups to be assessed and allows for increased flexibility through all planes of movement.

Spine

The spine can move through all planes of movement (frontal, sagittal, midsagittal, and transverse) by bending, twisting, and leaning. Some common ailments of the spine include lower back pain, bulging disc (vertebral disc bulges outward), and herniated disc (tear in the wall of the disc). Lower back pain is common among clients and can often be due to increased weight gain in the midsection. If disc problems are present, it is important to have these properly diagnosed by medical personnel and to modify the exercise sessions accordingly. Some twisting movements may need to be avoided, and clients may need to spend most of their time using machine weights where they are properly supported. High-impact activities should be avoided.

Irregular curves
The three irregular curves of the spine include the following: lordosis (excessive curvature of the lumbar spine), scoliosis (S-shaped lateral curvature of the spine), and kyphosis (excessive curvature of the thoracic spine). Lordosis can cause discomfort in the lumbar spine and make many high-impact exercises uncomfortable; standing for long periods of time can also be painful. Scoliosis and kyphosis can cause difficulty in completing full range of motion, and certain exercises may need to be off limits for the client. Utilizing machine weights to properly support clients with extreme cases of lordosis, kyphosis, and scoliosis may also be necessary, as well as avoiding high-impact activities.

Aerobic and anaerobic energy systems

The anaerobic pathway uses the ATP-PC system and glycolysis to generate ATP. The ATP-PC system uses up any stored ATP in the muscles, which is not a significant amount, and only supplies about a 10-second burst of activity. Glycolysis uses carbohydrates to create ATP by partially breaking down glucose and does not need oxygen to complete the process; lactic acid is its byproduct. Glycolysis provides some usable energy for a few minutes before aerobic energy pathways take over the process. The aerobic pathway uses oxygen to break down carbohydrates, proteins, and fats to create usable energy for the body and is used to fuel endurance activities. After the first few minutes of an exercise session, as heart rate climbs and ventilation increases, plenty of oxygen becomes available in the bloodstream in order to convert glucose to ATP. For the purposes of anaerobic training, recovery times should be kept short (30 seconds or under) in order to gain the most benefit.

Normal acute response to cardiovascular and resistance training

The normal, immediate response to cardiovascular exercises is for heart rate and blood pressure to increase and ventilation to increase. This increase transitions the body from anaerobic to aerobic pathways of energy by filling the body with oxygen that can be converted to energy. As the body becomes more conditioned to cardiovascular training, differences can be noted in the timing of heart rate; primarily, resting heart rate lowers and it takes more intensity to bring the heart rate up into the ideal training zone for the client during an exercise session. The normal, immediate response to resistance exercise is for heart rate and blood pressure to increase, but they do not stay elevated (unlike the cardiovascular response).

Normal chronic response to cardiovascular and resistance training

The chronic response to cardiovascular training lowers resting blood pressure and heart rate. In addition, it takes more intensity to increase heart rate and blood pressure, so the client is able to exercise for longer durations or higher intensities. Lactic acid is cleared from the muscles more effectively, and in longer endurance sessions (e.g., marathons, etc.) can be converted to usable energy. Repetitive resistance training helps to condition the anaerobic system and also can increase the size of the muscle fibers. Depending upon the mode used in resistance training, strength, power, or muscle definition can be increased. Over time, the client can experience positive benefits such as weight loss, increased coordination, increased strength, and increased motivation for exercise.

Warm-up and cooldown

The warm-up helps prepare the body for exercise by slightly increasing heart and blood pressure to move blood to the working muscles. The warm-up should move from general to specific so that the entire cardiovascular system is warmed up but also the specific muscles are warmed up prior to use. A complete warm-up helps to prevent injury and also increases flexibility and joint range of motion. A proper cooldown helps slow heart rate down to prepare to come back to resting levels; skipping the cooldown can lead to dysrhythmias because of a slight decrease in venous return. The warm-up and cooldown are integral parts of an exercise routine and should not be ignored. They promote safety in training, increase range of motion and flexibility, and prepare the body to enter and exit the training session.

Overtraining

Normal fatigue for a few days after training is a normal experience for a client; if pain is persistent (lasting longer than one week) and/or sharply painful, the client may be overtraining or have an injury. Overtraining can be observed with the following signs and symptoms: fatigue, feelings of moodiness and irritation, depression, lack of enthusiasm about future workouts, and sleep problems. In addition, a client may notice an abnormally elevated heart rate during cardiovascular exercise, a decrease in overall performance, and lowered immunity to sickness. The client who is overtraining may not be doing this under the personal trainer's supervision, but on her own time. It is important, therefore, to be aware of all the aspects of a client's training program and know what she is doing on her own for workouts.

Physiological adaptations during continued exercise at submaximal levels

Continued submaximal exercise can produce positive effects in the nervous system, muscular system, and skeletal system. The nervous system responds most quickly to training, and motor units in the spine begin to activate faster and more often, becoming more efficient in stimulating muscle fibers to begin working and adapting to exercise. A client can experience increased strength and power very quickly as a result of training. The muscle fibers begin to grow in size and increase in number as a response to continued resistance training. Bones also begin to increase in density, which is particularly helpful for women as they age. Within the cardiovascular system, the heart becomes more effective at pumping blood, resting heart rate and blood pressure are lowered, and capillaries increase to allow better perfusion of oxygen and carbon dioxide. Continued resistance training also increases mitochondrial and capillary density in the muscles and more effectively uses oxygen for energy. Maximal exercise should be reserved for testing purposes as it doesn't provide additional benefit but may actually encourage injury.

Rest as part of the training cycle

Adequate rest between training sessions is an integral part of the training cycle. It allows bodily systems to recover from the stress of exercise and to be prepared for the next session. Without adequate rest, the client will find it more difficult to lose weight, increase performance, and be motivated for workouts. Inadequate rest will lead to overtraining and possible injury. It is up to the personal trainer to explain the importance of rest to the client because often the initial reaction is to exercise more often or longer than necessary, hoping to achieve results in less time. Particularly if the client has a history of being sedentary, he may hope to make up for "lost" time.

Differences in training for muscular strength and endurance

Muscular endurance can be achieved through increased repetitions and decreased weight; muscular strength can be achieved through decreased repetitions and increased weight. It depends upon the client's goals as set forth by the results from pre-exercise screening and testing as to whether muscular strength or endurance should be achieved first. Most often, an increase in muscular strength is the area that needs attention first so the client can successfully complete activities of daily living.

Changes in blood pressure

When moving from a standing to a sitting or a lying position, blood pressure and heart rate decrease. When moving from a lying position to a sitting or standing position, blood pressure and heart rate increase. When sitting or lying down, gravity acts on the splanchnic region to lower aortic pressure and thus blood pressure and heart rate. Blood pressure at rest can remain low through continued exercise as the arteries and veins become more pliable, and blood can flow through with less effort.

Isotonic/isometric and concentric/eccentric muscle contractions

An isometric contraction occurs when the muscle contracts but does not change shape, whereas an isotonic contraction occurs when the muscle contracts and shortens to overcome the weight of a specific load. The isotonic contraction occurs in two phases: the eccentric (lengthening) phase and the concentric (shortening) phase. An example of an isometric exercise would be performing a plank, because there is tension in the muscles but they are not shortening or lengthening. An example of an isotonic exercise would be a push-up because various muscles are shortening or lengthening to complete the movement.

Major muscle groups

The major muscles of the body include the following: trapezius (runs along the upper back and neck), rhomboids (in between the shoulder blades), pectoralis major and minor (chest, beneath the collar bones), latissimus dorsi (lower back), deltoid (shoulder), biceps (runs along the front of the arm at the humerus), triceps (runs along the back of the arm at the humerus), rectus abdominis (beneath the pectoralis muscles), internal and external obliques (beside the rectus abdominis), erector spinae (run along either side of the spine), gluteus maximus (beneath the latissimus dorsi), quadriceps group (runs along the front of the leg at the femur), hamstrings group (runs along the back of the leg at the femur), abductors (runs along the outside of the leg at the femur), adductors (runs along the inside of the leg at the femur), gastrocnemius (runs along the back of the leg at the tibia and fibula).

Major bones

The major bones of the body and their range of motion include the following: skull, cervical vertebrae, thoracic vertebrae, lumbar vertebrae, pectoral girdle, sternum, ribs, humerus, radius, ulna, carpus, metacarpals, phalanges (hands), hip bones and sacrum, coccyx, pubic symphysis, femur, patella, tibia, fibula, tarsus, metatarsals, phalanges (feet). It is important for the personal trainer to understand the major bones in the skeletal system so that she can properly inform and educate a client on what bones are connected to the musculature that a particular exercise is working.

Joint classifications

There are six types of joint classifications: hinge (flexion/extension; knee), pivot (rotation of one bone around another; neck), ball and socket joint (flexion/extension, external/internal rotation, adduction/abduction; hip), saddle joint (flexion/extension, adduction/abduction, circumduction; thumb), condylar or ellipsoidal joint (flexion/extension, no rotation; joints between metacarpals and phalanges), plane or gliding joint (connection of flat bone joints; clavicular joints).

Agonist/antagonist muscle movements

The agonist muscle initiates movement, while the antagonist muscle opposes that movement. For instance, in a bicep curl, the biceps brachii is the agonist muscle that initiates the eccentric part of the curl, and the triceps brachii acts as the antagonist muscle. When doing resistance exercises, it is very important to work within the accepted range of motion; hyperextending joints or muscles will increase injury and could also cause misalignment of the bones through repetitive hyperextension. If a client injures himself early on in the training regimen, it could negatively affect his motivation and faithfulness to exercise.

Hypertrophy, atrophy, and hyperplasia

Hypertrophy of a muscle refers to an increase in the size of the muscle fibers. In turn, this increases client strength which can positively impact her activities of daily living. Atrophy occurs when a muscle group is not worked effectively or often and refers to a decrease in the size of the muscle fibers. This decreases strength and ability to perform normal tasks. Atrophy can be a result of overlooking the training of a particular muscle group or can be the result of an accident. Hyperplasia refers to an increase in the number of muscle fibers. Resistance training can be used to overcome atrophy and increase hypertrophy of the muscle fibers. Hyperplasia has not been well documented in humans; however, with proper resistance training and rest periods, muscles can recover more quickly from the micro-tears that are a result of continued training.

Cardiovascular fitness, muscular strength and endurance, and body composition

Cardiovascular fitness creates a healthy heart by lowering resting blood pressure and heart rate and increasing elasticity of arteries and veins. Muscular strength and endurance help clients perform activities of daily living with ease and crosses paths with cardiovascular fitness in that both areas can be used to prevent disease or reduce its symptoms. Cardiovascular fitness and muscular strength and endurance training also help reduce body composition, which in turn lowers the risk of disease for the client. It is the best option for the client to work within all areas of fitness in order to achieve the best results.

Components of fitness

There are five components of fitness that help an individual become well-rounded in his training: body composition (ratio of fat-free to fat mass), muscular endurance (how long the muscle can continue contracting), muscular strength (how much resistance the muscle can overcome in a contraction), aerobic capacity (endurance of the cardiovascular system), and flexibility (ability to stretch). These five components should be measured on a semi-regular basis, and one should not be emphasized over the others; the exception is when one area is significantly weaker than the others.

Contraindications to exercise testing

If a client experiences any of the following issues, she should not undergo exercise testing: an EKG reading that indicates a recent acute cardiac event or ischemia; unstable angina; uncontrolled dysrhythmia of the heart that has other symptoms present; severe aortic stenosis; uncontrolled heart failure with accompanying symptoms; acute myo- or pericarditis; history of aneurysm or suspicion that patient might have an aneurysm; any acute infection where fever, body aches, or swollen lymph nodes are observed. For these clients, exercise testing poses a risk that is not outweighed by any benefits. If a client experiences any of the following issues, she may still go through the exercise testing process as long as the benefits of the testing will outweigh the risks involved: left main coronary stenosis, moderate stenotic valvular heart disease, abnormalities in electrolyte balance, severe hypertension (systolic BP of >200 mmHg and/or diastolic BP of >110 mmHg), tachydysrhythmia or bradydysrhythmia, hypertrophic cardiomyopathy (any other forms of outflow tract obstruction), neuromuscular/musculoskeletal/rheumatoid disorders that will be aggravated by exercise, high-degree AV block, ventricular aneurysm, uncontrolled metabolic disease, chronic infectious disease, mental or physical impairment that leads to an inability to exercise properly.

Laboratory testing procedures for body fat analysis

There are several available procedures for assessing body fat. Skinfold measurements, circumference measurements, and body mass index are often used because they are easily accessible in the field by personal trainers and other allied health professionals. Skinfold measurements pinch specific sites on the skin to take a measure of subcutaneous body fat. The measurements are put into an equation with a body fat percentage resulting. Circumference measurements assess different body sites with a measuring strip, then are added together. The body mass index takes different factors (age, weight, height), puts them in an equation, and gets an approximation of body fat percentage. Of these three field calcula-tions, the skinfold measurements provide the most accurate body fat percentage; however, when dealing with clients who are sensitive about their weight or are extremely obese, girth measurements or BMI might be more helpful, even if it is not as accurate. The drawback for BMI is that it can't distinguish between fat and fat-free mass; a muscular person and an obese person could have a similar BMI. In the laboratory, more accurate methods can be used such as BOD POD (uses air displacement to measure body fat and is most accurate), bioelectrical impedance (measures resistance to electrical flow through the body to determine fat and fat-free mass), infrared (uses an infrared light to determine fat and fat-free mass), and DEXA (measures bone mineral density). These methods, however, are expensive and not able to be used in the field very easily.

Exercise tests

The following tests can be used easily in the field: body composition (skinfold or circumference measurements), cardiovascular fitness (1.5-mile run test), muscular strength (1 RM or multiple RM test), muscular endurance (push-up test), and flexibility (sit and reach). Tests should be performed so that the energy system responsible for that test is not completely taxed prior to the test. Additionally, adequate rest should be taken in between each test.

Field tests vs. laboratory tests of body fat analysis

Field tests and laboratory tests for body fat assessment vary quite a bit. Field tests typically require minimal equipment and are fairly simple to perform with a client. Laboratory tests are more accurate but also require expensive equipment to carry out and are not necessary for every client. Very few clients need the specificity of laboratory equipment, whereas exercise science studies need that exactitude in calculations. A personal trainer needs enough information to set accurate goals for the client to achieve health benefits, and field body fat tests are able to provide that.

Appropriate fitness assessments for special conditions and injuries

The fitness assessment should take place after the client's paperwork has been assessed. Any special conditions or injuries should be noted prior to exercise testing. The appropriate tests should be suited to the client; for instance, if the client is overweight or out of shape, the running test may not be appropriate, but the 6-minute walk test is appropriate. If the client has a shoulder injury, the push-up test would not be appropriate, but the abdominal curl-ups would work. If all five areas of fitness can be assessed without aggravating an injury, that should be the goal of the personal trainer in order to have a well-rounded view of the client's overall health.

Order of fitness assessments

Body fat analysis should be carried out first as it is the least invasive and taxing for the client. Cardiovascular tests should be completed first in the order for exercise screening because they use the largest muscle groups. Putting other tests prior to this one would cause undue fatigue. Muscular fitness assessments should come next. When determining what weight to use for the RM tests, be sure to give 3–5 minutes of rest between each of the submaximal RM warm-up repetitions. Flexibility tests should come last because all of the muscles have had time to warm up, and injury can be prevented.

Interpretation and explanation of test results

The results from all fitness measurements should be compared to accepted health standards to see where the client's current fitness level is. Next, these results should allow the personal trainer to know the order of training based on the area of greatest need. The results should also be explained to the client in a way that he can understand, so he is motivated to meet his goals. If any of the absolute or relative contraindications are present prior to or after beginning exercise testing, testing should be stopped immediately and the client referred to a physician.

Referral to physician

If exercise testing indicates that the client should seek a physician before continuing, the personal trainer should highly encourage it. If the client has an uncontrolled issue and is not currently seeing a physician, the personal trainer should be prepared to recommend some who are in the immediate area. Once medical care is established, the personal trainer should have an ongoing relationship with the physician to maintain the best care of the client. It is also important for the physician to know what is happening in the exercise program as it may change or affect the care she is providing.

Importance of heart rate and RPE

Heart rate and RPE help the personal trainer keep track of how hard the client is working. RPE has been shown to correlate highly with the client's response to exercise. It is appropriate for the personal trainer to check client heart rate and/or assess RPE multiple times throughout the exercise session. The personal trainer must be sure to record heart rate and RPE; this will provide another way to keep track of how the client is progressing in his level of fitness. Understanding these variables will also help the personal trainer know when an exercise is too challenging and needs to be modified or when it is not challenging enough.

Normal and abnormal acute responses to cardiovascular exercise

A normal response to cardiovascular exercise is for heart rate and systolic blood pressure to increase but for diastolic blood pressure to remain mostly unchanged. An abnormal response to cardiovascular exercise is indicated by the following: onset of angina or angina-like symptoms, drop in systolic blood pressure of >10 mmHg from baseline measurements, dramatic rise in blood pressure (systolic >250 mmHg, diastolic >115 mmHg), shortness of breath/wheezing and/or leg cramps, indications of poor gas exchange (light-headedness, confusion, pallor, nausea, etc.), heart rate fails to increase with exercise intensity increase, obvious change in the rhythm of the heart, client asks to stop the exercise, onset of severe fatigue, or the equipment fails to respond.

Circumference measurements

The standard circumference sites taken for measurement are as follows: abdomen, arm, buttocks/hips, calf, forearm, hips/thigh, mid-thigh, and waist. Measurements should be taken with a plastic, flexible measuring tape; the tape should not press hard enough on the skin to make an indentation. Go through each measurement site once, and then repeat a second time. The circumference waist measurement can be used to assess risk for disease. For females, <70 cm is associated with very low risk, 70–89 cm with low risk, 90–109 cm with high risk, and >110 cm with very high risk. For men, <80 cm is considered very low risk, 80–99 cm low risk, 100–120 cm high risk, and >120 cm very high risk. Higher circumference values indicate more fat storage and thus greater risk for disease.

Skinfold measurements

When selecting skinfold sites, the personal trainer must decide how many sites will be measured; there are options for 3 and 7 site measurements. All measurements should be made on the right side of the body with the client standing. The personal trainer should pinch the skin in each site, placing the calipers around the pinched skin halfway between the base and crest of the fold. The calipers should stay in place while reading the measurement, but no longer than 1–2 seconds. Duplicate measurements should be taken to ensure accuracy; it is best to rotate through the measurements so the skin can regain normal thickness and texture.

Circumference measurements vs. skinfold measurements

Circumference and skinfold measurements follow a similar pattern in measurement sites; however, the circumference measurements use a tape measure rather than skin calipers. Circumference measurements would be ideal for the client who is extremely overweight, where the skinfold measurements might be more difficult to obtain. Both circumference and skinfold measurements have similar accuracy in assessing body fat and are easy to complete in the field for personal trainers.

Assessing safety in muscular strength, endurance, and power tests

When choosing what tests to have a client perform, the personal trainer needs to keep in mind several variables. If the client has joint problems such as arthritis or impaired mobility due to disease or spinal misalignment, the personal trainer must pick a proper version of each muscular test and decide when modifications are appropriate. A test should never be performed when a client is currently injured; the client must wait until he is recovered in order to achieve the best test results. When training for resistance, a normative acute response for the client includes an increase in blood pressure and heart rate to divert blood to the working muscles.

Dangers of training for flexibility outside a joint's proper range of motion

When training a client to meet flexibility goals, it can be dangerous to exceed a joint's range of motion because damage can be done to the ligaments and tendons. In addition, if a client has led a sedentary life and is not in the habit of stretching, the muscles will be tight and stretching will need to progress in a gradual fashion. Consistency is key in increasing flexibility; keeping a stretching regimen as a regular part of the exercise session reinforces the importance of stretching for the client as well as helps her reach her flexibility goals.

Assessment of kyphosis, lordosis, and scoliosis

The personal trainer can elect to complete a postural analysis with the client. For kyphosis, the personal trainer can observe whether there is curvature of the thoracic spine and/or the neck slightly pushed forward. Lordosis can be observed by noting whether the client has an anterior or posterior tilt to the pelvis. Scoliosis can be observed by having the client stand against a wall that has horizontal lines on it. Observe whether the client tilts to the right or the left; one shoulder will appear farther away from the horizontal line than the other. If lines are not present on the fitness center wall, lines can be drawn on a poster board to hang on the wall. Knowing whether any of these issues are present will help the personal trainer troubleshoot potential range-of-motion issues.

Informing a client of exercise testing results

A positive way to inform a client of exercise testing results is to begin by letting him know his strengths first. For instance, if a client did well on the abdominal curl-up test, but poorly on the 1 RM bench press test, he is doing well in the area of muscular endurance, but needs work in the area of muscular strength. The trainer should tell the client he is doing well in the area of muscular endurance but will need to increase his results in the area of muscular strength. The client now has a positive foundation to begin making changes in areas where he had negative test results. Conversely, a negative way to inform a client of exercise testing results is to let the client know about his weak areas first. Often, this is demoralizing to the client if he is not naturally inclined to be motivated towards reaching fitness goals. While it is important for the client to understand the truth of where he stands physically, it needs to be done in a way that reinforces the notion that he is capable of lasting change.

When the client has her testing results positively explained to her, and goals set to help fix her weak areas of fitness, it gives the personal trainer a way to continually assess the client's progress. In reassessing goals, the client is clearly able to see how the training is helping her, which leads to stronger motivation to stay faithful to the new habit. Positive progress also helps her to see the benefit of exercising on her own time and also gives her the ability to begin making additional goals regarding other habits she wants to change. Seeing change in one area leads to a positive feeling of being able to take control of life habits she previously thought she was incapable of doing.

Creating achievable goals

In order to create the most effective goals, the personal trainer must do the following: listen to what the client is saying, assess the initial paperwork, and assess initial exercise capacity. As the trainer listens to the client, she will hear what the client wants to see changed about himself. This is useful because when the goals are created, the client will recognize he has ownership in the process. Initial paperwork will show whether there are pre-existing conditions that need to be addressed by specific types of exercise. The initial exercise testing will further reveal weak areas in fitness that need to be addressed.

Using client goals to create a workout regimen and troubleshoot negative behaviors

A client shares she wants to lose 20 lbs; in addition, the personal trainer realizes she may have an uncontrolled metabolic disease. The client struggles with completing the 6-minute walk test and the 1 RM test, has an abdominal circumference measurement of 115 cm, but does well on her sit-and-reach and push-up tests. The trainer can strategize to create a primary goal that increases the client's overall cardiovascular fitness and muscular strength, then share with the client how reaching these goals will help her to lose the weight she wants. Additionally, the personal trainer shares with the client that she should seek medical attention because her paperwork indicates she may have an uncontrolled metabolic disease. In the event the client seems reluctant to show up on time to sessions, or go along with the personal trainer's suggestions, there are several options available for the personal trainer. The personal trainer can choose to verbally encourage the client in her progress, have monetary penalties for missing training sessions without prior notice, create a reward system for goal maintenance, etc. The trainer should be creative with these options and choose one that fits the personality of the client.

Reassessment

Goals must be reassessed at regular intervals to measure progress. This can be done in a variety of ways; for instance, a personal trainer might take notes during each individual training session, but then reassess each goal with a fitness test every 6–12 weeks depending on the difficulty of the goal and how many sessions the client has completed. The personal trainer gains valuable information that can be passed on to the client. When the client understands his progress, he is motivated to continue wholeheartedly in the sessions.

Exercise Programming and Implementation

ACSM risks and benefits

Exercise guidelines for otherwise healthy adults include the following: in general, adults should do fitness-related physical activity 3–5 days per week, do leisure-related physical activity 2–3 days per week, and sit sparingly. The following exercise guidelines refer to seniors: in general, they should acquire 30 minutes of moderate physical activity on most if not all days of the week and should consult a physician before moving to a more vigorous program. Flexibility and resistance training should be included on several days each week. For children, the following guidelines are applicable: have at least 60 minutes and up to several hours of physical activity that is age appropriate on most to all days of the week. Activity should be moderate to vigorous and should take place in 15-minute increments. Activities lasting longer than 2 hours should be discouraged. For women who are pregnant, the following guidelines apply: moderate physical activity should be accumulated on most to all days of the week if there are no contraindications to exercise present. In addition, regular exercise is encouraged; if a woman was previously sedentary, light intensity exercise is encouraged. Exercise in the supine position is discouraged after the first trimester. It is important to understand the ACSM risks and benefits of exercise for adults, seniors, children/adolescents, and pregnant women because it allows the personal trainer to know what she can incorporate for exercise testing and prescription purposes. These guidelines serve as a road map for the trainer and client to see what the acceptable norms are for exercise. Knowledge of the risks and benefits helps the trainer know what will be most appropriate for the client for each session.

Clients medically cleared to exercise with chronic disease

Many patients have a chronic disease but have been advised by their doctor to exercise. In such cases, specific guidelines apply to their exercise prescription. Patients who have arthritis are encouraged to perform cardiorespiratory training 3–5 days/week (20–60 min, large muscle groups), resistance 2–3 days/week (1 set of 3–20 repetitions, 8–10 exercises), and flexibility 5–7 days/week ideally (15–30 sec per stretch, all the major muscle groups, 2–4x each). Patients with diabetes mellitus are encouraged to perform cardiorespiratory training 3–4 days/week (20–60 min), resistance (2 days per week minimum with 48 hours of rest in between, 1 set of 15–20 repetitions for each major muscle group), and flexibility (every day ideally). Patients with dyslipidemia are encouraged to perform cardiorespiratory training 5 or more days/week (40–60 min, primarily large muscle group aerobic activities), resistance 2–3 days/week (1 set of 3–20 repetitions, 8–10 exercises), and flexibility 5–7 days/week ideally (15–30 sec per stretch, all the major muscle groups, 2–4x each). Hypertensive patients follow a similar protocol as those with dyslipidemia with the following alterations: cardiorespiratory activity on 3–7 days/week (30–60 min), and resistance training should be in combination with aerobic activity using lower resistance and higher repetitions. For obese patients, cardiorespiratory training should begin initially with a moderate intensity, 45–60 min/session on 5–7 days/week. Obese patients may use resistance guidelines that apply to otherwise healthy adults.

Individuals with metabolic syndrome may use the same guidelines as otherwise healthy adults unless there is a negative immune response to exercise; otherwise adequate rest may be needed prior to continuing. Individuals with osteoporosis should incorporate the following: resistance activities 2 days/week with the load directed over the long axis of the bone (1–2 sets of 8–10 repetitions), flexibility training on most to all days of the week, and cardiorespiratory activity that is not high impact. Individuals with peripheral artery disease should have an extended warm-up (5–10 min) and walking should be the main form of cardiorespiratory activity (3–5 days/week). Resistance training should be complementary to other activity, not instead of the activity. Patients with pulmonary disease should have a minimum of 3–5 days/week of cardiorespiratory activity, and resistance guidelines are the same as otherwise healthy adults.

Physiological responses during exercise that may require a physician

If a client experiences any of the following responses during exercise, the personal trainer may want to refer her to a physician: angina or angina-like symptoms, excessive drop in systolic blood pressure when workload remains constant, shortness of breath and/or excessive cramping in the legs, lightheadedness, confusion, nausea, cyanosis, heart rate does not increase even though exercise intensity increases, an obvious change in heart rhythm. Any of these symptoms could indicate something more serious, and should be referred to a physician for follow-up.

Modifications during initial fitness assessment

Certain clients may require modifications in order to complete the initial fitness assessment. If a client has a disease that affects his range of motion or ease of movement, it may be more beneficial to modify assessments or skip some assessments because the risk of injury outweighs the benefit to the client. In addition, clients who are obese may not be able to complete assessments for muscular endurance and strength or flexibility due to their weight. In such cases, it is acceptable to begin with the recommendations allowed for their population group.

Functional fitness and sports-specific training

Functional fitness refers to fitness exercises that easily translate to real life experiences and help avoid injury in those situations. For instance, for a client who experiences low back pain whenever she does things during the day that require twisting of the spine, it is helpful for the personal trainer to incorporate movements that require twisting of the spine through different planes of movement and with varying resistance modalities to strengthen that area and train it in a new movement pattern. Sports-specific training emphasizes speed, strength, power, and endurance in athletic situations and also includes training specific to the sport in which the client participates. The average client does not necessarily need to engage in sports-specific training.

Balance training

Balance training becomes more important as clients age, and is especially important if clients have diseases such as arthritis. Balance can be included as a separate section of the workout, or if the client is more advanced, it can be combined with other exercises. An example of balance training can be to simply balance on one leg for a certain amount of time. An example of a combined balance and resistance move could be to do a one-legged bicep curl. In addition, balance can be included in cardiovascular training by having clients walk up and down stairs without the use of the railing or walking backwards on an indoor track. Modifications for balance exercises can include providing support for the client by allowing him to hold on to the personal trainer's arm, wall, or railing.

Sports-specific training in power and strength

Sport-specific training for power tends to emphasize explosive movements. This can be achieved through jump training (plyometrics) and through resistance training. Such examples would include jumping hurdles or doing jump squats, and using lighter weights but lifting as quickly or "explosively" as possible. Understanding the anaerobic system allows the personal trainer to work for the goal of power more effectively by utilizing rest periods to full capacity. Strength training involves methodically increasing weight while doing fewer repetitions in order to gain strength. For sports-specific strength the entire body is worked, but the muscles needing to be strengthened for sports performance are given special attention.

Anaerobic vs. aerobic training

Aerobic training uses oxygen to convert food nutrients (primarily carbohydrates) into usable energy. Any time exercise continues after 2 minutes, the aerobic system kicks in. The anaerobic system is the first responder to exercise, and it also converts food nutrients (primarily carbohydrates) into a fuel source, but it does not use oxygen to do so. Anaerobic exercise can refer to short bouts of activity and includes resistance and plyometric training. Aerobic exercise tends to refer to endurance activities such as running or bicycling.

Precautions to take during extreme weather conditions

When extreme weather conditions are present, special care should be taken if exercise testing or training must take place outside. If conditions are hot and humid, it is important that the clients are well-hydrated prior to beginning exercise and are given plenty of opportunities to re-hydrate during exercise. They should be wearing clothing that is moisture-wicking and avoid wearing cotton if at all possible. Clients should be given adequate rest periods. Clients should be observed for signs of heat stroke or heat exhaustion. When conditions are cold and humid, the same instructions apply but with a few modifications. Clients should layer clothing that is moisture-wicking so they can remove it as their body warms up. Additionally, the warm-up should be lengthened to warm up the muscles adequately. In either situation, personal trainers should monitor the clients closely, as they will not always be assertive when they need hydration or if they feel light-headed or dizzy.

Training at moderate and high altitudes

At higher altitudes, it is important to ensure that clients remain hydrated. When a client feels cold, she may not necessarily feel thirsty. Higher altitudes can quickly cause dehydration if the client is waiting until she feels she needs a drink. Feelings of fatigue can also be increased as less oxygen is binding to the hemoglobin molecules in the client's blood. Frequent breaks may be in order, and if the client is traveling to moderate or high altitude and intends to exercise, she must be aware that she may not be able to exercise at the same capacity. She also needs to schedule water breaks even when she is not thirsty. It is important to drink water throughout the day so she is adequately hydrated for her exercise session.

Recording client progress

Recording client progress at the end of each exercise session gives the personal trainer a small picture of how the client is doing from session to session. At the time of reassessment and re-testing, the trainer can then compare results with session notes. This gives both the trainer and the client a full picture of progress. In addition, if keeping in contact with a cooperating physician, it is necessary for the personal trainer to provide ample documentation for liability reasons and so the physician stays as informed as possible.

Choosing appropiate exercises for specific goals

The personal trainer bases each exercise session around one or more of the client goals. With primary goals, it may be necessary to center the entire session around that one goal. With secondary goals, it may be effective to group them together for a session. The client will be more invested in each workout if he knows what goals are being worked on and why. If he can see how the exercises he is doing will help him reach his goals, he will also have increased motivation to continue faithfulness to the exercise routine.

Program design and session and long-term goals

Program design must be specific to where the client's current level of fitness lies. It will not be a beneficial experience for either the client or the trainer if session goals and long-term goals do not match. Session goals should be building blocks that help the client reach the overall goals and thus must be closely related to the overall goals. The program design must properly reflect both the session and overall goals. It is beneficial for the trainer to recognize in both written and verbal form the specific goals for each session.

Interval, continuous, and circuit training programs

Interval training for cardiovascular fitness involves changing speed or grade at various time intervals at which the activity is performed. Continuous training involves staying at a similar speed or grade throughout the entire activity, and circuit training combines cardiovascular and resistance training. Each of these three types of training can be advantageous for cardiovascular fitness. For individuals who were previously sedentary, continuous training is helpful when it is maintained at low to moderate intensities because it will build their endurance, encourage weight loss, and condition their heart rate. Interval training can provide challenges and increase caloric expenditure while still training the client's cardiovascular system. Circuit training combines resistance activities with cardiovascular activities and helps build strength as well as endurance. The drawbacks to these types of training are similar to anything else; if continued for too long, clients will reach a plateau in their performance. Additionally, if one is emphasized over the others, cardiorespiratory fitness or muscular fitness may suffer.

Interval and circuit training could be disadvantageous for a client if the primary goal is to increase her endurance. When doing these types of activities, the client may have to stop the exercise sooner than if a continuous mode of activity was used because the intensity is more difficult. If endurance is the primary goal, it should be attended to first. As endurance increases, interval or circuit training may become more appropriate to include in the training regimen.

Energy systems used
In continuous training, the aerobic system is the primary responder. It is also the primary energy system used in interval training, provided there is no break taken between intervals. With circuit training, either the anaerobic or aerobic system can provide the primary source of energy. When circuit stations are done for less than 2 minutes with at least 30 seconds to 1 minute of rest between stations, anaerobic pathways supply the energy through the ATP-PC and glycolytic pathways. If stations are rotated with less rest, or clients stay at the station for more than 2 minutes, the aerobic system becomes the primary energy pathway.

Rest within circuit training
In circuit training, rest performs a very important function if the goal is to tax the anaerobic system and cause it to be the primary function. The rest periods between stations cause the anaerobic system to "reload" and be ready to function in the next set of exercises. It is important for the personal trainer to understand that rest plays a large part in the training of the anaerobic system.

Relation of ADLs to long-term fitness goals

When the personal trainer is assessing and creating long-term client goals, it is important to assess how the client feels about his normal life activities. The personal trainer can question him about his leisure time, whether he feels he is physically able to do what he enjoys, or whether any common activities (i.e., sitting or standing for long periods of time) cause unnecessary discomfort. The personal trainer must incorporate exercises that address these issues as they directly correlate to the client's quality of life. Increasing his quality of life allows the client to see that exercise can enable him to do what he enjoys, and it helps him desire to continue seeing those benefits. Activities of daily living can have both short- and long-term goals that relate to them.

Activity and training recommendations for different goals

For general cardiovascular and strength benefits, clients can follow the general guidelines as set forth by ACSM for cardiovascular and muscular fitness and flexibility. For losing weight, it is recommended that clients expend at least 2000 kcal per week in physical activity. For gaining weight, clients need to focus on resistance training for hypertrophy. In addition, for both clients who wish to lose weight and who wish to gain weight, diet plays an important role. In losing weight, caloric ingestion must be regulated and decreased from when they were sedentary. In gaining weight, caloric ingestion must be increased, but it must come from nutritious foods. To improve fitness level and increase athletic performance, clients can focus on specific variables, such as hypertrophy, power, endurance, and speed training as best fits their personal goals. The key with this type of clients is to make sure each workout is challenging and not too comfortable for them.

Advanced methods of resistance training

When a client has given evidence that she is ready for advanced forms of resistance training, the personal trainer can introduce methods such as super sets, Olympic-style lifts, plyometrics, pyramid training, drop set training, contrast training, complex system, lactate tolerance system, or negative set system. Only when the client has moved easily from easy to complex movements in traditional resistance training models should she move on to more difficult resistance training. Olympic-style movements train clients for quick, explosive movements that lift heavier weights. Plyometrics, also known as "jump training," trains for speed and power through different styles of explosive jumps. Pyramid sets begin with high volume and low weight, then increase to low volume with high weight through each subsequent set. Drop set training is a system that uses the same exercise performed to volitional failure in one set, then the weight is lowered and the exercise is repeated. Contrast training combines strength and power training by completing one exercise until volitional failure; a similar movement is then per-formed with a lighter weight but faster pace. Complex training com-bines agonist/antagonist exercises to fatigue a certain muscle in or-der to encourage hypertrophy. The lactate tolerance system has the goal of finishing a predetermined workout in the shortest amount of time possible. The negative set system encourages the exerciser to lift a heavier weight than normal, control the eccentric contraction, and have a spotter assist her with the concentric contraction.

Fitness components related to motor skill

Agility refers to a client's ability to explosively perform several different power movements one after another and in opposing directions; for example, zigzagging. Balance refers to a client's ability to control his body position while either standing still or moving. Reaction time means the client is able to react quickly to exercise stimulus or verbal instruction and change his movement pattern accordingly. Speed is quickness of movement, and power refers to explosive contractions of the muscles. Coordination is the client's ability to do all the aforementioned components so that effective movement occurs.

Contraindications for squats, planks, reverse crunches, and plyometrics

If a client has bad knees or shoulders or back, is morbidly obese, and is unfamiliar with exercise in general, the following types of exercises should be avoided: squats, planks, reverse crunches, plyometrics. Clients need to be started with exercises that are simple before moving on to exercises that are more complex. In addition, clients may need the extra core support that standard resistance machines give before moving on to body-weight exercises that are unsupported. Beginning with these sorts of exercises increases the risk for unnecessary injury.

Contraindications for yoga, PNF, static stretching

Yoga might be contraindicated if the client has greatly reduced flexibility, has an injury, or has had joint or back surgery. In these instances, it is wise to consult the client and assess whether the potential benefit would outweigh the risk. PNF or static stretching might be contraindicated for the client if joints are inflamed; if stretching causes excessive pain; or if she currently has an infection, a vascular or acute injury, joint instability, or a disease that affects the tissue being stretched. If in doubt, consult medical personnel before beginning a stretching regimen.

Contraindications for high-intensity, high-impact cardiovascular exercises

High-intensity, high-impact cardiovascular exercises should be avoided in clients if they have a chronic disease that compromises their joints, an acute injury, acute infection or sickness, or if in general the client has any physical issues that may be exacerbated by beginning a high-intensity regimen. For most clients, moderate physical activity is sufficient for health benefits and disease reduction. The personal trainer must assess the benefits/risk ratio for his client.

Recommendations for overall fitness

Healthy adults and seniors
In general, the client should engage in cardiorespiratory activity 3–5 days/week, resistance training 2–3 days/week, and flexibility (ideally) 5–7days/week. Each activity should emphasize the major muscle groups. Cardiorespiratory training should occur ideally at a range of 12–16 on the RPE scale, and resistance exercise should occur at a range of 19–20 RPE with the intent to reach volitional failure. Stretches should be held for 15–30 seconds each, with each muscle group being stretched 2–4 times at each session.

Healthy children and adolescents
Children should accumulate 60 minutes to several hours of moderate and vigorous physical activity on most days of the week. There should be several periods of activity during the day that last 15 minutes or more, and all activities should be age appropriate. Extended periods of activity that last longer than 2 hours are not encouraged during the day due to heat considerations.

Healthy pregnant women
In pregnant women who are healthy, 30–40 minutes of physical activity on most to all days of the week are encouraged. Women who were sedentary prior to becoming pregnant can begin an exercise regimen that is light. Exercise in the supine position after the first trimester should be avoided due to slightly obstructed venous return that lowers cardiac output and could cause orthostatic hypotension.

Adults with cardiovascular disease but medically cleared to exercise
If clients have a chronic heart disease that is stable, they generally need an extended warm-up (5–10 minutes), resistance exercises 2 days/week that include all the major muscle groups (clients should perform 1 set of 10–15 repetitions to moderate fatigue and use 8–10 different exercises; weight should be increased at a rate of 2–5 lbs per week for arms and 5–10 lbs per week for legs), and cardiovascular activity 3–4 times weekly (in addition to an increase in daily total energy expenditure) that is moderate intensity. For the greatest benefits, 5–6 hours of cardiovascular activity per week is recommended. Stretching all the major muscle groups (15–30 sec each, 2–4 stretches per muscle group) daily is encouraged.

Adults with metabolic syndrome but medically cleared for exercise

For clients who have a metabolic syndrome but are medically cleared for exercise, their goals should include the following: cardiorespiratory activity 3–4 days/week, lasting 20–60 minutes, at an intensity of 50–80% of their HRR. Resistance training should emphasize lower resistance and lower intensity: 1 set of 10–15 repetitions for each of the major muscle groups, increasing to 15–20 repetitions. Stretching of all the major muscle groups (15–30 sec each, 2–4 stretches per muscle group) should be emphasized on a daily basis.

Adults with chronic pain and arthritis but medically cleared to exercise

For adults who suffer from arthritis or other joint pain, their exercise prescription is as follows: cardiorespiratory (3–5 days/week, 20–60 min duration, large muscle groups emphasized), resistance (2–3 days/week, 1 set of 3–20 repetitions, 8–10 total exercises that cover all the major muscle groups), flexibility (preferred: 5–7 days/week, 15–30 sec each, 2–4 stretches for each major muscle group). Overstretching should be discouraged; morning exercise depends on a client-by-client basis, based on whether they find it helpful or not.

Importance of accurate medical history

For clients who are pregnant, children and adolescents, and the generally healthy population, it is always necessary to have an accurate medical history. This decreases the personal trainer's liability by allowing her to prescribe exercise that will avoid exacerbating medical issues. The trainer will also understand what medications the client is on and how they may impact exercise. Additionally, the personal trainer will be aware of potential triggers for worsening any existing medical conditions.

Exercise modifications

When an exercise is too challenging or not challenging enough, the personal trainer should give a modification that will make it more appropriate for the client. It is the personal trainer's responsibility to observe the client and ask questions to make sure the intensity or the type of exercise is appropriate for the client; some clients have a "pain is gain" mentality and may not volunteer that the exercise is too difficult for them. Likewise, clients new to exercise may not realize if an exercise is too easy for them; they may simply appreciate that they don't feel horrible as they exercise. The personal trainer must educate her clients on the benefits of an appropriately challenging workout.

Components and appropriate flow of an exercise program

An exercise session should start up with an adequate warm-up of the large muscle groups that will also increase the heart rate and prepare the body for what is to come. Depending upon the client, static stretches may be appropriate after the warm-up. Resistance activity should come next, so the client is not too fatigued to be paying attention to proper technique, appropriate weight choice, and personal trainer cues. Next should come cardiovascular activity, followed by a cool-down, and static stretches.

Exercises for major muscle groups

The following exercises would be appropriate for the major muscle groups: chest (push-ups), upper back (double arm row), abdominal muscles (abdominal curl-ups), lower back (good morning), quadriceps group and hamstring group (weighted squats), calves (calf raises), shoulders (shoulder raises), biceps (biceps curls), and triceps (triceps dips).

Monitoring response to exercise

During exercise, there are various ways that a personal trainer can monitor a client's response to exercise. The RPE scale is an efficient way of assessing whether the workload is too challenging or not challenging enough for the client. Paying attention to physical signs of distress, such as labored breathing, pallor, dizziness, or sharp pain, can also be indicators that something more serious may be occurring.

Maximum heart rate and heart rate reserve

In order to find the maximum heart rate, simply take the client's age and subtract it from the number 220. The resulting number is the age-adjusted maximum heart rate. To find the heart rate reserve (HRR), take the client's age and subtract it from 220. Take the resulting number, and subtract the resting pulse from it. This is the heart rate reserve. If training according to a percentage of the client's heart rate reserve, multiply the HRR by the percentage desired for training, then add the resting pulse to it. **Example:** A 60-year-old client needs to be trained at 70% of his HRR, his resting pulse is 65: 220 – 60 (age) = 160 (age-adjusted maximum heart rate); 160 – 65 (resting pulse) = 95; 95 x .70 = 66.5 + 65 (resting pulse) = 131.5 bpm. This client should have the goal of 131 bpm for training at 70% of his HRR.

Target heart rates for different medical considerations

Depending on the chronic condition that the client has, a specific training zone will be based on her HRR. Cardiac patients should have a goal of training up to 85% of HRR. For managing hypertension, training from 40% to 70% of HRR is recommended. For clients with arthritis, it is recommended to train within 50% to 85% of HRR. Diabetic clients should train within 50% to 80% of HRR. For clients with dyslipidemia, it is recommended to train within 40% to 70% of their HRR. For obese clients, initial exercise should have the goal of being within range of 40% to 60% of HRR; progression to higher intensities (50% to 75% of HRR) is recommended. For clients with osteoporosis, it is recommended to pursue non-impact activities at 40% to 70% of HRR.

Periodized training

Periodized training allows the personal trainer to focus on goals such as endurance and hypertrophy with a client while avoiding overtraining. For example, a period of 12 weeks can be broken down into 3 periods of 4 weeks in each period. Through these different periods, the trainer varies the client's intensity, frequency, and duration of exercise so that a plateau is not reached, but maximal hypertrophy and endurance is attained. Chance of injury is reduced because the client is rotating training styles and also which muscles are receiving the most training. Periodized training also helps those clients concerned with increasing different exercise variables such as speed, strength, and power.

In a periodized training schedule, the personal trainer can vary the goal within each period so that muscular power, hypertrophy, endurance, and strength can be achieved without reaching a plateau. For the goal of power, high-intensity, short-interval exercises should be included with the goal of most movements being explosive rather than static. Moderate-intensity sessions should be in between the power sessions to promote recovery. For hypertrophy, resistance training should be with a moderate-intensity weight, 10–15 repetitions, with rest of 30–60 seconds between sets. Endurance activities can be coupled with hypertrophy training and should be between 30–60 minutes for 4–6 days per week at moderate intensity, or 30–60 minutes 2–3 days per week for higher training intensities. Strength training should be done with higher resistance than hypertrophy training. The goal should be 2–3 sets of 6–8 repetitions, where the client feels tired with the last 2 repetitions. Additionally, exercises should be specific to the client's sport goals if they have any.

Repetition maximum test

The 1 RM test measures the greatest amount of resistance that the client can move through a full range of motion while still in control of the weight. This can provide a measure of either upper body or lower body strength. The benefit of knowing the client's 1 RM allows the personal trainer to more accurately estimate submaximal resistance loads with which to begin training. An example of the 1 RM test for the upper body is a bench press; an example of the 1 RM test for the lower body is the leg press.

Resistance exercises to build strength

Resistance exercises can help build muscular strength and endurance. When using the proper types of exercises, a client is able to more easily complete activities of daily living, deter rapid bone loss, and reduce the risk for joint disease. Resistance training works along with cardiovascular training to decrease fat mass and increase lean mass. Resistance exercises break down the muscles by creating micro-tears in the tissue; the proper recovery period helps to rebuild those tissues and increase strength and hypertrophy.

Effects of cardiovascular training on activities of daily living and endurance activities

Cardiovascular training helps the heart to pump blood more effectively. As such, resting heart rate begins to lower and resting blood pressure begins to lower. During exercise, heart rate and blood pressure take longer to increase as the body becomes more efficient with the workload. Clients will notice the longer they are committed to an exercise routine, the more daily activities they will be able to complete with less pain or fatigue involved. Clients will also notice better quality of sleep and feel more energetic. For endurance activities, clients will notice that they can exercise for longer periods of time, increase their speed, and overall adapt to training stimulus more quickly.

Effects of exercise on motor skills and coordination

As clients exercise, they will notice a positive effect on motor skills and coordination. With specific training in each of the following areas: resistance, flexibility, cardiovascular, and balance, clients will have increased quality of life. Coordination and motor skills are improved when speed and balance activities are included in the training regimen. Balance training can be incorporated in resistance training (e.g., completing a bicep curl while standing on one leg) or in cardiovascular activities (e.g., power skips or bicycling) and trains clients to use their fine and gross motor skills to complete the movement. The more movements are practiced in an exercise session, the more efficient clients will become in performing them, and their motor skills and coordination will continue to improve.

Demonstration of expected movement patterns

To ensure the client understands exactly what to do for an exercise, the personal trainer needs to physically demonstrate the movement pattern as well as provide verbal and nonverbal cues. It is never appropriate for the trainer to assume the client understands based on verbal instruction alone. An example of a verbal cue is to give instructions for how to complete an exercise. An example of a nonverbal cue would be personally demonstrating the exercise or helping the client complete the movement.

Demonstration of proper range of motion

Demonstrating proper range of motion helps the client to remain free from injury. One resistance exercise that is often done incorrectly is the lat pull. People will typically pull the bar down behind their neck and head. Although the glenohumeral joint can rotate 360 degrees, it is not advisable to train by bringing the arms behind the head in this manner. Proper form requires lowering the bar in front of the face and neck but not leaning back away from the bar. Performing this exercise improperly often leads to overuse injuries in the shoulder joint that could become serious enough for medical attention.

Benefits of using several different resistance modalities

Using several different resistance training modalities allows the trainer to see what the client enjoys the most. This also gives the client a taste of the variety resistance training can offer. Additionally, muscles can be trained in different ways depending on the goal of strength, hypertrophy, endurance, or power, and it becomes less likely that a plateau will occur for the client. Examples of different resistance modalities include the following: variable resistance devices, static resistance devices, kettle bells, dynamic constant external resistance devices, etc. It is necessary for the personal trainer to always keep her eyes on the client during the performance of each movement. Spotting is appropriate and requires verbal and nonverbal cues to ensure the client is performing each movement as safely as possible.

Nontraditional resistance training activity

For some clients, nontraditional resistance training may be in order; this can include stability balls, balance boards, resistance bands, medicine balls, and foam rollers. These pieces of equipment are useful for clients who are rehabilitating from injury, are elderly, are incapacitated in any way, or need to work on their balance. Additionally, it provides a way to change a movement and make it more complex so as to increase the intensity of the workout for clients. Using this type of equipment is also considered functional training and helps clients achieve ease of movement and greater strength in activities of daily living.

Dangers of the Valsalva maneuver

The Valsalva maneuver occurs when a client holds his breath during a resistance or cardiovascular exercise. This is dangerous because it causes a sharp increase in blood pressure and heart rate which can lead to the client becoming light-headed or dizzy and passing out. Clients need to learn to breathe appropriately during cardiovascular exercises and during the eccentric and concentric phases of resistance training in order to avoid the Valsalva maneuver.

Biomechanics of resistance training, yoga, and running

In resistance training and yoga the spine will move through all planes of movement in a variety of ways including bending, twisting, and stretching and will also move through the frontal, sagittal, and transverse planes. Yoga uses almost exclusively isometric training, while resistance training may utilize isometric or isokinetic training. Both resistance training and yoga can exert compressive forces on the spine, and care must be taken to protect vulnerable areas. During running, the spine should stay relatively stable with little to no twisting and no bending or stretching, and should only move through the frontal plane. Compressive forces will also be present for the spine during running activities. Joints may go through flexion, extension, circumduction, abduction, adduction, or hyperextension for running, yoga, and resistance training.

Negative effects when training is ceased

If a client stops training for an extended period of time, her muscles begin to atrophy, and gains that are made in both the cardiovascular and muscular systems are lost. Clients may begin to notice that they have aches and pains returning and that range of motion becomes more limited. They will lose the ability to complete with the least amount of effort tasks that require increased levels of coordination and may become short of breath with a lower amount of exertion. When they begin training again, clients can increase their abilities and functional performance within the cardiovascular and muscular systems. The rule of thumb is "if you don't use it, you lose it."

Overtraining

The following are signs that the client may be overtraining: fatigue, moodiness, unenthusiastic about workouts, difficulty sleeping at night, and irritation. If these signs are obvious in the client to a great extent, it may be necessary to refer the client to a physician. Overtraining can result from a desire to get in shape faster by exercising longer and harder than is necessary and not utilizing rest periods. It can also be the result of poor self-image or an eating disorder. It is necessary for the personal trainer to educate the client on the dangers of overtraining and how it can be avoided.

Improper form and technique

Using improper technique and form, whether performing cardiovascular or resistance-type activities, can be detrimental to a client's health. It can cause overuse or acute injuries, both of which impede a client's progress in reaching his health goals. Injury may give a client misgivings about continuing an exercise routine and lower his motivation to become healthy if he feels he is just going to be injured. Additionally, improper technique lessens the benefit of the activity being done because the muscles are not being trained in an appropriate fashion. Also, inappropriate motor patterns for the movement are recorded in the client's mind, and he will have to "unlearn" the wrong technique in order to learn the right technique. It is always more beneficial to learn the correct technique the first time.

Appropriate exercise clothing

When exercising in outdoor conditions, the client must pay attention to the appropriate clothing for outside temperatures. If it is hot and humid outside, cotton is not an appropriate clothing choice because it will not wick away excess moisture from the skin. It is best to avoid wearing a hat, as that will also hold in heat. When exercising in a cold environment, the client must layer her clothing and have a moisture-wicking layer closest to the skin. As she gets hot, she can remove clothing accordingly. The appropriate tennis shoe must also be chosen for whether cardiovascular exercise is prescribed or whether speed or resistance training is prescribed. A thinner-soled shoe is required for plyometric or resistance training, and is also more helpful for training in balance issues.

Learning styles

It is important for the personal trainer to remember that the client may not have a learning style that corresponds with his own. In such circumstances, the trainer needs to be informed on how best to train that client in a way that will make sense with her learning style. For instance, a kinesthetic learner may need to not only have verbal instructions, she may need to do a practice try of the movement before actually beginning a set. Additionally, a visual learner will learn best by watching the trainer go through a complete range of motion with the movement, and an auditory learner will rely heavily on verbal cues.

Properly spotting a client

When spotting a client, the personal trainer must stand either behind, beside, or in front of the client. The appropriate position is dependent on the movement being completed. The trainer should ask permission prior to touching the client; all touch should be professional and with the intention of providing assistance for the movement if necessary.

Determining whether an exercise session should end or continue

If a client is working at an intensity higher than is beneficial for him, it can be evidenced by labored breathing, inability to talk, flushed face, or complaint of sharp pain. If an exercise is stopped, the personal trainer needs to assess whether the client can continue working out after a short break. If client heart rate lowers significantly and client feels able to continue, exercise can continue. If the client still feels faint or exasperated following the break, the session may need to be terminated.

Normal and abnormal response to exercise

In a healthy adult, the normal response to exercise is increased heart rate and blood pressure as blood is shuttled to the working muscles. In an adult with chronic health issues, heart rate and/or blood pressure may rise too quickly and cause negative symptoms that may cause the exercise session to be terminated. The personal trainer must make sure adults with chronic conditions begin exercising according to their appropriate protocols.

Improper use of cardiovascular equipment

One example of improper technique when using cardiovascular equipment would be hunching over from the waist or gripping the bar on the treadmill. Both of these issues can cause poor posture and reduce the number of calories being used. Additionally, the client may become light-headed or dizzy because she is compressing her diaphragm by leaning over, which leads to insufficient breath intake and thus hyperventilation to get more air and oxygen to working muscles.

Improper technique for resistance machines, free weights, and stability equipment

When doing any type of resistance activity, form must be prioritized in order to avoid injury. With a resistance machine, any movement that causes the client to arch his back would be an example of improper technique and may indicate that he is using too much weight. For free weight exercises, if the client struggles to complete the move in general, or begins to lean backward in order to complete the movement, this is also improper technique. With stability equipment, any time it is used for something other than its intended purpose to promote balance, it is being used improperly.

Improper stretching techniques

An example of improper technique for partner stretching would be for the partner to force a muscle to stretch farther than it is capable of stretching due to muscle tightness or impaired range of motion. With static stretching, the client must be sure to hold the stretch rather than bouncing in the stretch, as this would promote muscle injury. With dynamic stretching, it would be improper for the client to move a joint outside of its normal range of motion in order to heighten the stretch.

Assessment of client's understanding

There are various ways that a personal trainer can assess the client's understanding of the movement patterns. Once the trainer has finished demonstrating and instructing the client on how to do a specific exercise, she can ask if what she has said makes sense. Additionally, she can ask if the client has any questions prior to beginning the exercise. Finally, it will become clear during the course of the movement whether the client has understood the instructions and demonstration. If he performs the movement improperly, he lacks clear understanding of what was asked of him.

Effective communication of proper technique and feedback

When giving feedback to a client regarding proper technique for exercise, the personal trainer should utilize as many avenues as possible to communicate. The trainer can verbally explain the proper technique needed. He should follow this with a demonstration of the movement pattern. The client should then attempt the movement pattern one time without any additional weight or resistance of any kind. As the client is performing the movement, the personal trainer should be spotting her and providing verbal cues the entire time. Throughout the process, the client should be allowed to ask questions and encouraged to do so. When giving feedback regarding client performance, the trainer should begin with what the client has been doing correctly so far and any ways she has improved since the initial exercise testing. Additionally, once the trainer has given feedback to the client, the client should be allowed to ask questions. In areas where the client is still deficient in performance, the trainer should share with her a plan for improvement.

Modification of exercise programs for healthy individuals

For pregnant women, if any absolute contraindications are present, exercises may not be an option for them. If any of the relative contraindications are present for a pregnant woman, modifications will be necessary to her typical routine. Additionally, as she progresses further into her pregnancy, her center of gravity shifts forward, requiring exercise to be modified for comfort. For adults, seniors, children, adolescents, and pregnant women, exercise may be modified for an acute injury or sickness, extreme discomfort associated with an exercise, or extreme temperatures. If a client is dehydrated, exercise should be stopped altogether.

Benefits of modifications for clients with chronic disease

When clients with chronic disease are cleared to exercise, modifications may be necessary for a variety of reasons. When first beginning an exercise routine, clients may need extra modifications in order to feel successful with what they are doing. As they progress through their workout plan and begin to meet their goals, exercises may have to be modified to become more challenging to reach future goals. Modifications also provide a range of choices for clients so they can have some autonomy in choosing parts of their workout routines. Additionally, clients who are exercising under doctor's orders must be given a progression of exercise that takes their recent medical history into account. Heart rate should be regularly monitored, and their level of exertion (using the Borg RPE scale) should be closely followed also.

Avoiding training plateaus

Specificity
Specificity of exercise refers to training that upholds a specific goal; for instance, strength training requires different protocol than speed training. When training for strength, an example of specificity would be to create a particular goal for each session that focuses on strength for a certain area. One session might focus on core strength, while the next focuses on lower body strength. Specificity helps to avoid a training plateau because the personal trainer is keeping track of when the client reaches the training goals for strength in a particular area. Once this goal is reached, a new goal can be made, with the training sessions specifically corresponding to it.

Progressive overload

The term progressive overload refers to progressively overloading a bodily system for the purpose of exercise training. For instance, one way of achieving progressive overload for endurance cardiovascular training would be to increase distance run by a half-mile per week. This helps the client to achieve the overall goal of a specific distance while also training the cardiovascular system to function more efficiently. However, since the distance is being increased, it keeps the body from becoming overly efficient and expending fewer calories at a distance that becomes too comfortable for training purposes.

Proper progression of exercise sessions

In order to reach the client goals at all, the personal trainer must continue to pay attention to proper progression of exercise from simple to complex. If training remains simple for the client, major cardiovascular and muscular gains will not be made. Additionally, a training plateau will occur once the body becomes overly efficient with an exercise routine. Changing one or more exercise variables (overload, specificity, duration, frequency) will allow the training plateau to be overcome.

Proper progression for developing strength in chest and legs

A proper exercise progression goes from simple to complex, single-joint to multi-joint exercises. As an example, proper progression for strength development in the chest might be as follows: assisted bench press on a resistance machine, bench press with free weights and an exercise ball, push-ups, burpees. For strength progression in the legs, an example of a proper progression would be seated leg extension, seated leg press, squat, side shuffle to a squat. The personal trainer should spot the client at each point of the progression.

Periodized training program to increase or maintain athletic performance variables

Periodized training programs are valuable because they allow training plateaus to be overcome, and they can be used to train an athlete for various parts of athletic performance. For example, the first period of training might be for strength and general cardiovascular fitness. The second period of training could be for speed and sport-specific skills with maintenance strength training. The third period of training could include the sports season, with maintenance for speed, strength, and sport-specific skills. The fourth period could include recovery, with limited endurance and strength training, while increasing exercise load towards the end of the period to prepare for the first period again.

Feedback regarding client's experience and assessment of progress

The personal trainer can gain an idea of the client's perspective of his training success through a variety of different ways. The trainer can verbally address the client and ask whether he sees he is meeting goals or not. The trainer can also create a checklist or survey for the client to fill out when goals are reassessed. At the end of the training, the personal trainer can ask the client to fill out a satisfaction survey to indicate the overall success of the program in his perspective.

Reviewing current goals and creating new goals

The personal trainer should assess the client goals at frequent intervals throughout the exercise program. For instance, if the client has contracted to work with the personal trainer for 40 sessions, it might be good to assess some of the minor goals every 5 sessions, while assessing the main goal(s) every 10 sessions. This gives enough time for change to take place, but the assessments are close enough together for the client to have the goals in mind during each workout. Once a goal is met, a new goal should take its place. The personal trainer and the client should both keep a log of when the goals are met and when new goals are created.

Leadership and Education Implementation

Communication with clients

There are various ways of communicating information with a client, and the personal trainer must find out which types of communication will be most beneficial for the client. Talking with the client over the phone is most beneficial if the client can be reached easily via telephone, although the personal trainer needs to understand the protocol of the fitness center for making such calls from her personal number. Depending on the fitness facility, email and text reminders for appointments can be appropriate if done through a business email or contact number. The personal trainer needs to be careful about sending personal information regarding the client through these avenues. Additionally, keeping an updated newsletter or website can be a means of communicating mass information to several clients; however, some clients may not use these sources as a general rule.

Verbal and nonverbal communication

Communication throughout the exercise session is both verbal and nonverbal. The personal trainer should give verbal instructions and encouragement to the client while also realizing that her body language will impact the client as well. It is important to make eye contact with the client and speak kindly and confidently to him so he understands that his personal trainer views his time and effort as important. The personal trainer should maintain a professional appearance at all times, maintaining a pleasant facial expression and keeping her attention focused on the client throughout the session.

Active listening

Active listening means that the personal trainer is listening to what the client has to say, looking at the client while she speaks, and asking questions at appropriate times to be sure of what the client means. Examples of active listening would be making eye contact with the client, jotting down notes regarding what the client is saying, ensuring he understands the client's request ("So what I understand you to mean is..."), and making any necessary changes to the workout routine based on the client's feedback.

Auditory, visual, and kinesthetic learning styles

An auditory learner can learn best through hearing something taught verbally; a visual learner needs to see something modeled for him; a kinesthetic learner needs to try something to understand it better. Typically, clients will have more than one learning style, and the style may vary between the different types of resistance training and cardiovascular training. One way to ensure the client has the best chance of understanding what is needed for a movement pattern is to describe the movement, model the movement for the client, then have the client complete a practice movement without any weight, or through a partial range of motion if the movement requires body weight as resistance.

Feedback

Feedback can be given to a client in a variety of ways. Evaluative feedback helps the client know what she is doing correctly and incorrectly in the movement pattern ("You are doing a great job of not allowing your knees to go past your toes, but make sure your toes are pointed forward."). Supportive feedback is a means of encouraging the client, perhaps through a difficult part of the workout ("I know it's tough, but we're almost through. Do you think you can finish 2 more laps?"). Descriptive feedback is clear and concise feedback that provides correction at the end of a movement pattern or session ("In future squat-type exercises, I want you to focus on squeezing the muscles of your gluteus to decrease pressure on your knees."). Feedback should be given to the client verbally at regular intervals, but also in written form when she is regularly evaluated for goal assessment.

Behavior change models

There are several different behavior change models, for instance, socio-ecological model, readiness to change model, social cognitive theory, and theory of planned behavior. With the socio-ecological model, the personal trainer understands that there are several different influences—personal characteristics, interpersonal relationships, community relationships, and societal influence—that combine to determine a person's pattern of behavior. The social cognitive theory proposes that personal characteristics, environ-mental characteristics, and behavior are all interconnected to each other and influence one another. The readiness to change model states that someone will pass through certain stages—precontemplation, contemplation, preparation, action, and maintenance—on the journey to change a behavior. The theory of planned behavior states that subjective norms, behavioral beliefs, and perceived behavior control all work together to cause some to have an intention to modify a behavior.

When the personal trainer understands what is motivating the client in each instance, he can more effectively help clients reach their goals. For instance, a client comes to a personal trainer and expresses in the initial evaluation that she has been amazed at the high rates of diabetes in the United States and so has decided to have her physical for the first time in several years. Upon having her physical, she found her blood sugar levels to be uncharacteristically high and thus decided she needed to lose some weight. The client realized she needed some assistance in reaching her goal and called a personal trainer. In this example, personal characteristics and societal influences worked together to cause the client to modify a behavior (socio-ecological model). Additionally, the client can be categorized as being in the preparation step of the readiness to change model. Finally, a problem in society caused the client to become conscious of her own health (subjective norms), assess her health, and determine it needed to change (behavioral beliefs and perceived behavior control).

Interference with client faithfulness to exercise programming

There are many things that can interfere with client faithfulness to an exercise program. If there is extra stress in a client's personal life, he may be less inclined to follow through with appointments. Work schedule and finances can also cause unfaithfulness to exercise. Falling back into poor nutritional habits and subsequently using the guilt associated with it to cause him to cancel training times is not uncommon. If a client feels that the personal trainer is not an effective communicator, or is not listening to him, he may express reluctance in moving forward with more sessions. Sometimes clients may fear not getting the results they want to see for themselves, may not manage their time wisely, or may not understand how to implement changes at home that will help them in their training sessions. It is the trainer's job to help coach clients through these issues.

Influencing a client avoid detrimental behaviors

A personal trainer can help a client avoid many of the pitfalls associated with outside stressors or relapses into previous poor habits by creating an "open door policy." The trainer can encourage honesty from the client while offering encouragement and constructive advice for avoiding common pitfalls. Providing compassionate accountability is very necessary for clients who may be more prone to fall back into sedentary habits.

Increasing client motivation to achieve fitness goals

Personal trainers can help clients reach fitness goals by working patiently with them, reminding them of their progress, and showing them objectively how they are reaching their goals. Trainers can also motivate clients by giving them rewards or awards for reaching their goals. Trainers can encourage clients to identify who can be a part of their social support network. Understanding how to motivate clients will enable the clients to be more faithful in reaching their goals.

Extrinsic and intrinsic reinforcement strategies

An extrinsic reinforcement strategy is an external way of rewarding or reinforcing positive client behavior. For example, if a client has recently reached a goal of losing 5 lbs, the trainer can positively reinforce and reward the client reaching the goal by giving her the opportunity to engage in only her favorite fitness activities for one session. An intrinsic reward or reinforcement would increase self-esteem; using the same example, if a client lost 5 lbs, her intrinsic reinforcement would be the increase in self-esteem.

Helping clients increase physical activity outside of exercise sessions

The client often understands the need to increase energy expenditure throughout the day in addition to the structured exercise sessions but may need help in understanding how to do this. The personal trainer can help by having the client describe a typical daily routine and then make suggestions on how to increase levels of activity. For example, the personal trainer might suggest the client take the stairs to the office instead of the elevator, park a little farther from the office entrance than normal, or take 5 minutes every hour of work to walk around the office a few times.

Healthy lifestyle

The personal trainer is very instrumental in helping the client understand what options are available for a healthy lifestyle. The personal trainer can take time at each session to discuss with the client the choices he has made throughout the week and how he can be more effective by choosing healthier options. The personal trainer becomes a mentor, source of accountability, cheerleader, and coach for the client and must encourage honest communication so the client can receive the best results of his programming.

Lifestyle management techniques and health coaching principles

One example of a lifestyle management technique is to have the client keep a food log and an activity log each week. The trainer can take the logs, make suggestions, and return the logs to the client to help promote change. Another example is to help the client identify sources of stress in her life and help create alternatives for managing it. Anytime the client can help in creating solutions to issues that stand in the way of well-being and health, the more likely she will be to follow through on the course of action.

Age- and fitness-appropriate levels of fitness education

The personal trainer needs to assess how clients receive information best. For instance, if some clients do not like to read, then giving them helpful articles might not be the best course of action. It is best to provide a variety of resources and opportunities for clients to learn more about fitness. For instance, newsletters, articles, short instructional videos, and verbal teaching can all be effective for client learning. Additionally, if there are some hands-on learning opportunities during the training session, this may work best for some clients. The trainer should be sensitive to any possible learning barriers clients may have and try to work around that. The more clients understand the whys and hows of the benefits of fitness, the more likely they are to stick with their program. The trainer must remember that fitness education is ongoing and not a one-time occurrence.

Influence of lifestyle factors on lipid and lipoprotein levels

A sedentary lifestyle, poor nutrition, and high stress levels are the most influential factors that cause unhealthy lipid levels for clients. When clients begin a normal exercise routine, begin to make healthy food choices, and learn to manage their stress more effectively, they notice a difference in their lipid levels. Genetics can play a role in predisposing a client to have high lipid profiles, but it takes unhealthy lifestyle choices to cause their genes to create poor health.

Fuel sources during exercise

Carbohydrates are used as the primary fuel source for exercise and are used at the onset of exercise. Only when carbohydrates are used up will fats and proteins be used for fuel. This takes a few hours of intense of exercise to accomplish; typically, the body wants to spare fat and protein to be used for other things. Fat and protein are more complex to break down into useable energy than are carbohydrates.

Body composition, body mass index, and lean body mass

Body composition refers to the ratio of lean body mass (or fat-free mass) to fat mass in a client. Body mass index is one way of assessing this ratio and relies on height and weight information to do so. Understanding a client's body composition allows the trainer to know if he is at a higher risk for certain chronic diseases and can determine what goals should be set for the client.

Typical fat distribution patterns in males and females

Overall, women tend to have a higher fat percentage than men do. Women also tend to carry more fat in their hips and thighs (gynoid or pear shape) than men. Men tend to carry more fat in their midsection (android or apple shape) than women do. Briefly speaking, epinephrine is the hormone that primarily stimulates the body to break down fat (lipolysis) for usable energy. Epinephrine stimulates lipolysis through beta receptors and inhibits it through alpha receptors; both of these receptor sites can be located on the same cell, but the receptor that has more locations will be the one epinephrine stimulates. Abdominal adipocytes are more sensitive to beta receptor activation by epinephrine than are adipocytes in the hips and thighs and are easier to break down. Women especially tend to have more alpha receptors in the hips and thighs, which promote adipocyte storage.

Anorexia nervosa and bulimia nervosa

Anorexia nervosa and bulimia nervosa are both eating disorders that arise from a client's dissatisfaction with self-image. Characteristics of anorexia include severe body image disorder, heightened fear of becoming fat, and excessive restriction of calories. Symptoms that can be observed in a client include the following: severe weight loss, strict dietary practices, and heavy exercise participation. Bulimia is characterized by eating excessive amounts of food (often in secret) followed by vomiting and possibly heavy use of diet pills or laxatives. Persons who binge eat may still be likely to be overweight, feel that they can't control their eating, have a long (failed) history of dieting, and are overall not happy with their bodies. Either of these diseases can result in hospitalization, suicide, and impaired relationships with others. If these conditions are suspected by a personal trainer, the trainer should discuss it with the client (or guardian if under 18) and highly recommend counseling.

Body composition and overall health

If a client is classified as overweight or obese, it can be an indicator of other health issues. In comparing body fat percentages in men, 3–5% body fat is essential for life, 6–10.9% is considered lean, 11–15.9% is considered fit, 16–19.9% is considered healthy, 20–24.9% is considered overweight and moderate risk for disease, and >25% is considered obese and high risk for disease. Likewise for women, 11–14.9% is considered essential for life, 15–18.9% is considered lean, 19–22.9% is considered fit, 23–26.9% is considered healthy, 27–31.9% is overweight and considered moderate risk for disease, and >32% is obese and considered high risk for disease. Waist-to-hip ratio is another easy way to classify the client's overall health in the field and to evaluate the current disease risk level.

Effects of diet, exercise, and behavior modification on body composition

Diet, exercise, and behavior all work together to either hurt or help a client's health by lowering body composition to a healthy or fit level. Eating a diet high in fruits and vegetables, low in simple carbohydrates, with healthy amounts of protein and fats, exercising the recommended 150 minutes per week, and managing and reducing stress levels helps the body to reduce fat storage, increase the effectiveness of the heart and circulation, and a host of other positive changes. The danger is for clients to think their health can be changed through only one or two of the variables rather than seeking positive changes in all three areas. Seeking change in only one or two areas will cause positive changes to either be slow in coming, or not happen at all. Clients will also be more likely to engage in unsafe practices; for instance, if they are only trying to modify their exercise habits without modifying their nutritional or stress habits, they may overexercise to unsafe levels to try and achieve their goal.

Hydration

Hydration plays an important role in exercise; it allows the cardiovascular system to function properly, keeps internal temperature at acceptable levels, and allows the body to perspire and cool itself effectively. If a client is dehydrated prior to exercise, the heart rate may increase too quickly to unsafe levels, and she will tire more easily with less effort. If a client doesn't replace the water lost through effort and perspiration following an exercise session, she can also dehydrate which will put excess strain on the cardiovascular system.

Proper nutritional and portion guidance

If a client is seeking help about establishing better nutritional habits and portion control, the personal trainer should be ready to provide resources. Some resources include ACSM dietary guidelines as found on their website, www.myplate.gov, and websites where clients can gain access to guidance on healthy meals they can make. Additionally, if a client eats out frequently, the personal trainer can show him how to navigate a restaurant website to find the healthiest option and how to have a backup plan for unexpected times of eating out.

Female athlete triad

The female athlete triad is comprised of the following three elements: disordered eating, osteoporosis, amenorrhea. Disordered eating leads to low levels of energy, osteoporosis leads to bone loss, and amenorrhea can lead to low iron levels or anemia. If a female has low iron levels or anemia, she doesn't have an effective way to make use of oxygen for energy because ultimately, hemoglobin production will be low and oxygen binds to hemoglobin. If she doesn't have enough hemoglobin production, she will not utilize oxygen appropriately for energy production. If bone loss occurs, females will be more likely to fracture or break bones and sprain or strain joints, ligaments, and tendons. If a female has low energy, she will not be able to put in or get out of her workouts the quality that is necessary for reaching her goals. Overall, if a female athlete suffers from the triad, her performance is hindered, and her health is put in jeopardy.

Inappropriate weight loss techniques

Clients who have been sedentary for a long time may try to see if they can lose weight more quickly than is healthy for them. They may try to overexercise in an attempt to lose weight more quickly, buy into fad diets or go on a completely liquid diet, take dietary supplements that are unsafe or interact negatively with other medications that they may be taking, or they may engage in anorexic or bulimic behaviors. Fad diets are often not based on sound scientific evidence and often encourage water or muscle weight loss rather than fat loss. Liquid diets may restrict calories to an extreme that is not healthy and does not provide enough calories to support bodily systems. As an industry, dietary supplements are not always regulated, and clients may not be getting exactly what they think they are with their supplements. With anorexic or bulimic behavior, clients may either overly restrict calories or binge and purge respectively, which greatly harms their overall health. The desire in these situations is to achieve a certain weight loss despite health risks that may be present, because the outcome seemingly outweighs the risks.

If a personal trainer suspects a client is engaging in unhealthy weight loss techniques, the trainer must attempt to educate him on why those behaviors are ultimately harmful to the overall goal of weight loss. The client needs to understand that it takes time to put the weight on, and it will take time to take the weight off. He also needs to realize what expectations are reasonable for his age and abilities; if the client is older, it is not reasonable to expect he will look like he did in his teenage years.

Kilocalorie content of fat, protein, carbohydrate, and alcohol

Fat has 9 kcal per gram, protein has 4 kcal per gram, carbohydrate has 4 kcal per gram, and alcohol has 7 kcal per gram. It is beneficial for clients to understand these values as the personal trainer educates them on how to read and interpret a nutritional label. Clients also need to be clear on whether they should be counting calories or grams for daily food intake.

Caloric intake

When a client's goal is to lose weight, the personal trainer needs to help her assess her current caloric intake first. Once this is assessed, the trainer needs to help the client restrict empty or bad calories and also replace them where appropriate with good calories that will provide sufficient energy. Additionally, the trainer needs to help the client think of ways to increase her overall energy expenditure. When a client's goal is to gain weight, the process starts out the same way but differs in that the trainer will help her increase calorically dense foods and also increase her snacks throughout the day. For both groups, however, nutrient density and timing are highly important so as to provide sufficient energy for metabolic demands.

Educating clients regarding ongoing, scientifically based information

It is important for the personal trainer to educate clients in an ongoing fashion about proper exercise through scientific sources. The trainer must understand that clients will hear contradictory information on a daily basis regarding exercise and dietary techniques, and it is important to keep them abreast of information that is true and factual. Education can take place casually, and articles can be given to clients at regular intervals at the training session or can be emailed to them regularly.

Providing opportunities for community involvement in exercise

The personal trainer can do a lot to provide opportunities for community involvement in exercise to help people participate. The trainer can help organize fun runs, provide group exercise sessions in the park, and organize classes to provide instruction on health and fitness. A community game day or field day can also be organized. The trainer can be active in writing for community blogs and internet sites to promote health and wellness.

Stress management for clients

The personal trainer can help the client assess areas of stress in his life. Stress can come on a daily basis or as a result of traumatic life events. The trainer should be willing to listen to the client's areas of distress and offer suggestions as well as including the client in the process of finding ways to manage those situations. It is important for the client to have ownership in the problem-solving process; that way he will be invested in the positive outcome. Additionally, the trainer can have a ready supply of professional staff to recommend to the client, for instance, licensed massage therapists, chiropractors, physical therapists, counselors, etc., to help in the process.

Legal, Professional, Business and Marketing

Stratifying client risk and obtaining medical clearance to minimize negligence

Negligence is defined as the breach of the duty of care between a professional and a client. If a personal trainer doesn't take time to stratify client risk and obtain medical clearance if indicated, she will be seen as negligent should anything happen to the client during the course of exercise programming. The personal trainer is obligated to do everything in her power to ensure the client is exercising in a safe environment with minimal risk to health and well-being; stratifying client risk and obtaining medical clearance meets this professional requirement.

Levels of risk stratification

The Health History Questionnaire enables clients to see specifically which risk factors affect them. For instance, the following risk factors could indicate coronary artery disease: hypertension, family history, high cholesterol, cigarette smoking, impaired fasting glucose, obesity, sedentary lifestyle. Additionally, risk factors can also be assessed during the exercise session. The following risk factors could indicate pulmonary, metabolic, or cardiovascular disease: pain or tension in chest, neck, jaws, arms, or other areas; dizziness; shortness of breath; orthopnea or nightly dyspnea; palpitations; ankle edema; known heart murmur; intermittent claudication; unusual fatigue or shortness of breath during normal activities. Clients can be stratified as low, moderate, or high risk based upon the aforementioned symptoms.

Medical clearance requirements

If a client answers yes to one or more questions indicating cardiovascular or metabolic or pulmonary disease and has a history of chronic disease, medical clearance is necessary to begin treatment through exercise. If a client answers yes to one or more of these questions, the personal trainer should take into account the health history as it is described by the client and should use his best judgment in recommending medical clearance or not. Generally, if the client was just barely placed in the moderate-risk category, but could be in the high-risk category very soon, medical clearance might be a good idea. Additionally, if the client responds poorly in the exercise testing, especially if she is unable to catch her breath or experiences heart palpitations, medical clearance is necessary.

Supervision for individuals who received medical clearance

Clients who have received medical clearance for exercise should be monitored continually during the exercise session. Additionally, they need to indicate how hard they feel they are working according to the RPE scale. These clients should never be left alone to exercise until they have come to a point where their risk factors are decreasing or it is deemed that they can exercise safely by themselves.

Continuing education

A personal trainer should keep abreast of changes and modifications within the field by attending regular continuing education. This can be done through taking classes that help to maintain certification or by receiving a degree in higher education. Training can be hands on, online, or in a classroom setting. The important thing is for the trainer to consider how this education will benefit her knowledge so that clients can ultimately benefit from it. The trainer should take classes that directly relate to the populations that she trains.

Scope of practice for certified personal trainers

The scope of practice for a personal trainer includes improving health and physical fitness as a means to prevent disease, health problems related to obesity, and premature aging. Personal trainers should not diagnose injuries or medical problems and should not attempt to perform the role of a physical therapist, athletic trainer, registered dietitian, or rehabilitation specialist. Although the trainer may understand certain concepts from other allied fitness professional fields, he is not licensed to practice them.

If a personal trainer practices outside the acceptable scope of practice, it can lead to negligence and false practice of other professions. A client may become injured when a personal trainer attempts to teach things she is not licensed to practice. Doing this increases the personal trainer's liability, and ultimately the client could sue for any damages that are a result of false practice. A personal trainer could potentially lose her business in such a situation.

Effective communication with allied professionals

If a client requires medical clearance to participate in a workout program, or has been referred to a personal trainer by a medical professional, it is appropriate to regularly communicate about the client's progress. The ideal ways for this to happen are through phone calls or postal service. Sensitive information should never be given through email or left on an answering machine, in order to protect patient privacy. The client also needs to be fully aware that information is being shared, and in the appropriate instances, sign a release of information.

Effective relationships with individuals in the greater health community

The personal trainer should always be aware that there are many different people invested in seeing a community grow in health and wellness. It would be to the personal trainer's benefit to network with like-minded medical and allied health professionals in the community by attending professional events and creating a strong referral system for clients to seek additional help that is outside the personal trainer's scope of practice. The trainer can partner with other professionals to provide special package pricing that includes multiple sessions of personal training combined with other professional services. Being active in the community and attending community health events is the best way for personal trainers to network with other health practitioners to reach a common goal.

Recommending other health services

When a personal trainer realizes that a client needs help in areas outside the trainer's scope of practice, the client needs to be referred. For instance, if a client needs more detailed information to help him nutritionally than is provided by the general guidelines found on www.myplate.gov, the client should be referred to a dietitian. If a client struggles excessively with finding solutions to stress management, and general guidelines for relaxation do not seem to suffice, the client should be referred to a life coach for further guidance.

CPR and AED

A personal trainer should maintain a current CPR/AED certification at all times. If a client becomes unconscious or stops breathing at any time, CPR protocol should be initiated. AED protocol should be initiated as necessary if there is more than one person at hand in a situation where a client collapses. If a personal trainer does not maintain a current CPR/AED certification, she could be held liable for practicing without a license.

Emergency procedures clearly delineated for the client

The personal trainer should make clear to the client proper procedure in case of emergencies. For instance, in case of a fire or inclement weather, the client should know where the exits are or where to seek adequate shelter. Whenever the fitness facility updates its procedures, it is the personal trainer's responsibility to ensure the client knows what to do. Additionally, the personal trainer should have on file permission from the client to call emergency services or a medical practitioner if appropriate.

Basic first-aid procedures

Exercise intolerance
If a client is experiencing exercise intolerance, a cooldown should be initiated immediately to bring the client's heart rate back down to resting levels. The client needs to drink adequate amounts of water to maintain hydration. The client should continue moving as necessary until heart rate returns to normal. If the client feels dizzy or overheated, he can sit down, but lying down is contraindicated. The client should be given some cool water, and a cold towel or compress should be applied to his neck to reduce body temperature. If the client is having trouble breathing due to chest pains, medical personnel should be contacted as it may be exercise-induced angina.

Exercise-related injury
If the client has an exercise-related injury, the client should be put in a sitting position and RICE (rest, ice, compression, elevation) should be followed for the injured area as needed. A medical practitioner should be immediately called. This information should be kept on file prior to any exercise sessions taking place so it can be accessed in the event of an emergency. The personal trainer should also have on file a client's permission to call emergency services in the event of an emergency if it's deemed necessary.

Client safety in the fitness facility

Client safety can be ensured by having them engage in exercises that correspond to their current fitness level. Clients should also be taught how to correctly handle resistance machines and free weights to avoid personal injury. They should also be made aware of facility rules regarding flow of traffic inside the facility, appropriate cardiovascular machine usage, and age requirements for using equipment. Clients should never use a machine they do not know how to use; this can be remedied by the personal trainer giving a comprehensive education on machine usage.

Injuries

There are several injuries that can be common complaints of clients, and it is beneficial for personal trainers to know how to work around them during an exercise session. Shin splints are characterized by pain along the outside of the leg starting right below the knee. A sprain is pain in the joint where a ligament has been overstretched. A strain is characterized by muscle fibers tearing because of being overstretched. Bursitis is inflammation of the bursa sacs. Tendonitis is inflammation or irritation of a tendon. A fracture is a break in a bone. Patello-femoral pain syndrome is localized pain in front of the knee. Low back pain is localized pain across the lower back in the lumbar spine and pelvis. Plantar fasciitis is inflammation of the fascia on the bottom of the foot and often results in heel pain and tenderness.

If shin splints, sprain, or strain occur during the course of exercise, ice should be applied immediately and the ankle or other joint elevated. The client should be encouraged to wrap the area in a compression sleeve and visit a medical professional. If a fracture occurs, medical help should be sought immediately. A client with bursitis and tendonitis should engage in non–weight-bearing cardiovascular activities, and resistance activities should utilize resistance bands. If a client has patello-femoral pain syndrome, medical clearance should be given prior to exercise, and non–weight-bearing cardiovascular activity should be the focus. Resistance activities should be focused around machine weights. For low back pain and plantar fasciitis, the warm-up and stretch segments should be extended, and myofascial release techniques should be utilized.

Contraindications to exercises of the major muscle groups

Even though some resistance exercises may be beneficial for many of the healthy population, they may be contraindicated in certain populations. For example, straight leg sit-ups and standing bent-over toe touches lose their exercise value for some people with neck and back issues because it places high compressional forces on the spinal column. Double leg raises can cause hyperextension of the lower back and place unnecessary stress on it, which is especially unneeded for clients who already have low back problems. Clients who are obese or have knee issues can cause undue stress by performing full squats. Overall, the personal trainer needs to assess potential exercise risk against reward when choosing exercises for the client.

Liability during emergency procedures

When an emergency situation happens and the client is directly under the personal trainer's supervision, the personal trainer is held liable for what happens to the client. The personal trainer is responsible for the client's safety while performing exercise, and if an emergency occurs within the fitness facility, the trainer must do her best to ensure the client's safety. The trainer must be up-to-date on fitness emergency procedures.

Common musculoskeletal injuries

When a client is not fit, there are some common musculoskeletal injuries that might take place. Although a trainer may do his best to monitor the client, there may be pre-existing weakness that predisposes the client to injury. Some common injuries are as follows: contusion (bruising) of the muscle, sprain or strain of the muscle, fracture (including stress fractures with overuse or poor footwear) of the bones. The client must also be aware of any predispositions to injury and know what to do about an acute injury if she is exercising on her own.

Management and first-aid during exercise

Common cardiovascular complications
If a cardiovascular event happens during an exercise session, the personal trainer needs to be aware of signs and symptoms that indicate it. The signs and symptoms are as follows: chest pain (or in head, neck, jaw, or arms), heart palpitations, hyperventilation, syncope, dyspnea, unusual shortness of breath during activities that typically do not bother the client, client's inability to speak. If any of these signs are present, the client may be suffering from exercise-induced angina, tachycardia, or asthma attack. Once exercise is ceased, if the symptoms do not go away, medical personnel should be called immediately. If the symptoms do go away, the client needs to seek medical attention prior to resuming exercise at the next session.

Common metabolic abnormalities
If a client is experiencing a metabolic abnormality during exercise, such as hypo- or hyperglycemia, the trainer should be aware of signs that indicate it. Signs indicating metabolic abnormalities are as follows: fainting, syncope, pale face, blurred vision, dry mouth, excessive sweating. For clients with known metabolic abnormalities, it is recommended for them to bring something to eat or drink in case of emergency.

Open wound

If a client has a wound that begins to bleed during an exercise session, the personal trainer should retrieve the first aid kit from the fitness facility. The client should be instructed to wash the wound with soap and water. The personal trainer should provide antiseptic and a band aid, and if necessary, help apply dressing. If the trainer needs to apply dressing, she should wear safety gloves that are included in the first aid kit.

Complications with musculoskeletal injuries

If the pain does not interfere with the client's ability to express himself clearly, the personal trainer should ask the client what the pain feels like (i.e., sharp pain or dull pain); if the injury occurs in one of the limbs, the personal trainer needs to apply the RICE method where appropriate. If the injury is to the head, neck, or spine, the personal trainer needs to initiate emergency or first aid procedures depending on whether first aid staff are available at the fitness center. The trainer should never attempt to move the client in this situation. Additionally, in order to remain within the accepted scope of practice, the personal trainer should ask the client to seek medical attention to treat the injury.

Complications of cardiovascular or pulmonary issues

If complications arise during an exercise session that could indicate cardiovascular or pulmonary issues, the client needs to first lower the intensity of the exercise, assess heart rate to ensure it is coming down from where it was, and ask the client questions about how she is feeling to assess whether she can talk. If the client can't talk, the intensity of the exercise needs to be lowered further. If heart rate remains erratic, or complications continue, the client needs to initiate cooldown. After cooldown, the trainer should stay with the client until heart rate is within 10 or fewer beats above the resting heart rate. Additionally, the client needs to drink some water.

Complications due to metabolic syndromes

If complications due to metabolic syndrome arise during an exercise session, the personal trainer needs to follow protocol similar to when complications are due to cardiovascular or pulmonary issues. The personal trainer must keep in mind that the client should never be left alone during this time. If reducing intensity of the workout helps the client reduce symptoms of complications, the trainer and client assess together that the client is able to continue the session, and no absolute contraindications are present, then the client can continue the session at the reduced intensity.

Ongoing evaluation of exercise equipment

A fitness center should maintain its equipment according to manufacturer guidelines. Manufacturer handbooks should be kept on file and easily accessible. Machines should be cleaned between client use throughout the day, and clients should be encouraged and instructed on how to clean the machines as they finish with them. All equipment should be checked daily to ensure it is in proper working order.

Ensuring safety policies and procedures are well-known among clients

A fitness center should have all exits clearly marked. Procedures for emergency situations (fire, inclement weather, etc.) should be clearly posted. Additionally, the personal trainer should go through the procedures with clients to ensure understanding. Clients should be trained on equipment usage to avoid injury and to have confidence in using the fitness center on their own. The personal trainer can assess client understanding of emergency procedures in a variety of ways. The trainer can verbally go through the steps of emergency response with the client. Additionally, he can practice the procedures with the client and allow time for questions regarding them. Ongoing assessment should occur. The trainer needs to be aware that it is his shared responsibility with the facility to ensure that the client understands all emergency procedures. The client should regularly practice all procedures.

If clients and staff don't properly understand how to act in an emergency situation, injuries can happen and unsafe behaviors can occur. Additionally, the fitness center can be held liable for any injuries or an unsafe situation that arises due to negligence. Procedures need to be put in place to safeguard the general well-being of the client/customer; if this is neglected, it becomes an issue of liability for the facility. If something were to happen to a client during an emergency that could have been avoided with proper training for the emergency situation, the fitness facility bears responsibility for that injury.

Necessary steps of emergency action plans

An emergency action plan for a fitness facility should consist of short, concise steps so clients and members can remember them. The emergency should be identified, a safe location should be designated in the proper area, and clients should be instructed on the proper path to that location. Emergency plans related to inclement weather (heavy thunderstorms or tornadoes) and fire should be in plain view and regularly practiced by facility staff and clients. Clients should be shown how to safely evacuate during a fire or seek appropriate shelter during a storm or tornado.

Spotting and assisting during exercise

Spotting and assisting clients with resistance activities allows the trainer to ensure they are using correct form and not lifting weight that is too heavy for them to be using. This is an active way to teach clients while allowing them to learn in an active way. Spotting and assisting also ensures weights don't get dropped or roll away and others in the vicinity won't be injured.

Continuing education

Continuing education is essential for the personal trainer to stay informed on the latest research and techniques in the field. It also allows for trainers to get to know other professionals in the field. It keeps training techniques from becoming stagnant and ensures they are up-to-date and based on the most recent supporting research. Continuing education also allows personal trainers to specialize in a certain area and become aware of where their professional interests actually lie. Continuing education must come through approved providers to ensure that professionals are receiving the same level of education.

ACSM requirements
For certified personal trainers, ACSM requires 45 hours of continuing education over every two-year period. Information for approved providers and courses can be found on ACSM's website (www.acsm.org)

Keeping up-to-date with current research

Current research allows personal trainers to maintain understanding of changes in their field of practice and the scientific research that underlies those changes. This becomes important because trainers need to understand the physiology of their practice and the reason for changes that need to occur. Understanding this information allows them to synthesize it and explain it to their clients in a way that makes sense, which ultimately helps maintain motivation and adherence to their exercise program because they understand why they are performing the specified activities.

ACSM's code of ethics

The ACSM code of ethics is a set of standards that govern all ACSM licenses. It includes guidelines on ethical practice, disciplinary issues, and personal trainers' responsibility to the profession and to the public they serve. Some examples of ethics related to personal trainers are the following: they must respect their clients at all times, they may not take credit for the work of other professionals in their field, and they must not claim the ability to perform services for which they are not certified. The ACSM code of ethics seeks to preserve a purity of conduct within all the professions it certifies.

Professionalism in dress and behavior

Personal trainers show professionalism in the way they dress by wearing professional attire that is not too short or too tight. Collared shirts are preferred, as well as proper footwear. The personal trainer should also maintain a professional manner with the client and other colleagues. Eye contact should be used during conversations, along with a pleasant facial expression. Where appropriate, refer to men as "sir" and women as "ma'am" unless the client indicates otherwise. When introductions are made, clients should be referred to as "Mr.," "Mrs.," or "Ms." unless instructed otherwise.

Ensuring professional activities are within scope of practice

The personal trainer should know the scope of practice and understand how to practice within its limits. Additionally, the trainer should have a copy of the scope of practice within view so the clients see it as well. This sort of transparency ensures an optimal working relationship between the client and trainer because the client knows exactly what to expect from the sessions.

Ethical business model

As the personal trainer is creating a business model, he must keep in mind that it is necessary to present the business honestly to prospective clients. To maintain this honesty, the personal trainer must be transparent towards clients and in professional relationships. Having started the business, the personal trainer must keep a detailed record of interactions with clients and of the results and outcomes of training sessions and goals. All clients should be treated fairly and without bias. If other employees are hired, trainers should follow the hiring regulations of their state. The trainer should also maintain continuing education credits for ethics courses.

Business models

There are a variety of ways a personal trainer can create a business. One way is to join a fitness center as an employee and trainer (corporation). In the corporation model, the trainer will start with a base hourly salary, and as she gains clients to train, commission will be added to the hourly rate. In this business model, the corporation is first held liable for anything that happens on its premises, and the trainer is already covered in a group liability insurance plan. Another business model is to own a personal business for training clients with either a partner (partnership) or alone (sole proprietorship). In the sole proprietorship, the trainer assumes all liability as well as all future planning and implementation. In the partnership, the owners can choose to equally be liable for and responsible for future planning and implementation, or they can choose to have limited liability (a limited partnership). If they choose limited liability, they also will have limited input in future planning and implementation. An S-corporation is an option that involves getting shareholders to back the business venture. In this scenario, the trainer and any subsequent employees are in essence working for the shareholders, and the shareholders provide the "start-up" money for the training business. This sort of business helps bring limited liability to the shareholders of the company, and profits and losses can be indicated on personal tax returns, not a business return. The business itself will not be taxed, but the individuals that make up the business will be taxed.

Components of budget kept on file

The personal trainer must have categories for business expenses and deposits. Examples of business expenses would be for equipment, gas, food, office supplies, rent for business space, liability insurance, loan payment, etc. As the business grows, the trainer may include categories for new employees and possibly a business savings account. It is important for the trainer to maintain records of expenditures and keep all receipts.

Policies for client protocol

The personal trainer should know ahead of time the policies for billing clients, client cancellation policy, late arrival policy, and payment methods. For instance, if all sessions are payable up front, the trainer needs to make this clear to the client. Similarly, the trainer needs to let clients know how they may pay for their sessions. In addition, if tardiness or cancellation past a certain time is unacceptable and results in a charge for the session, the trainer needs to let clients know this as well.

Objectives for the business

The personal trainer needs to meet with anyone who is joining the business venture and decide the mission and objectives for the business. They also need to define how they will assess whether they are meeting their objectives. Goals can be set weekly, monthly, quarterly, or yearly. Goals should be financial, personal, and related to client and business growth. One example of a business goal assessment would be to have each client complete a satisfaction survey at the beginning, middle, and end of session programming.

Mission statement

A mission statement describes the vision, values, and expected service for a business. An example of a mission statement for a personal trainer would be the following: _____
Personal Training Services believes in empowering individuals to take control of their personal health and wellness. We empower our clients by teaching and modeling fitness concepts that develop strength and health for the entire body.

Computer software for budget creation

Microsoft Excel or Access can be helpful in creating a budget spreadsheet for the personal trainer, although there are several different kinds of software available for this. Keeping a budget on a spreadsheet helps to minimize human error, especially when mathematical formulas can be programmed to keep track of expenditures and deposits. Additionally, keeping the budget in this manner is helpful for documentation as it looks more professional than a paper and pen budget.

Standards in career development

The personal trainer who chooses to start his own business needs to follow the standards of his state for hiring employees and enlarging the business. He also needs to have training standards set in place to ensure employees are as prepared as possible for entering the business. Employees should also be assessed a minimum of once yearly, and mentoring practices for new employees are highly encouraged. The personal trainer should make sure the business remains up-to-date with current trends and scientific information and remains active in the community to promote positive relationships with future clients.

Effective marketing

Effective marketing advertises the personal trainer's services accurately and reflects the benefit the client can expect to have as well as the cost involved. Effective marketing doesn't over- or under-sell the benefits expected from training and does not use exaggeration to make a point. The advertising may also show the introductory prices for training sessions; if an introductory promotion is being run, the date for the introductory period and the associated prices must be clearly marked.

Personal trainers can use a variety of ways to market their products and should be able to make use of them effectively. For instance, personal trainers may use brochures, business cards, webpages, blogs, video clips, and other forms of e-marketing to advertise their business services. Trainers need to ensure the medium they choose is appropriate to the setting; blogs and video clips may be more appropriate to show client testimonials of satisfaction, whereas brochures and webpages may be better suited to show pricing and packages available. The business card would be more appropriate for networking with other professionals or passing on their information for communication to clients.

Networking to promote services

It is wise for personal trainers to network throughout any venues available to them in order to grow their business. Some examples can be to attend networking functions hosted by other professions, feature their services in a press release, or advertise in conjunction with another group of services as a promotional package. For instance, a personal trainer and dietitian may advertise their services in one package if one of the professionals is more well-known than the other.

Evaluation of pricing

Personal trainers should evaluate their pricing on a yearly basis at the very least to determine whether it reflects the market value of their product and covers their expenses (rent, mileage, time involved, etc.). Depending on where a trainer chooses to practice, evaluations may need to occur more often.

Computer applications to create marketing materials

The personal trainer has an array of applications available to create marketing materials on the computer. Some examples include, but are not limited to, Microsoft Word, PowerPoint, and Publisher, and Adobe PDF. These applications can be used to create flyers, educational material, educational presentations, brochures, and articles. The personal trainer should be familiar with ways to use both print and web-based applications, and it would be to the trainer's benefit to learn how to create a business website and maintain it.

Negligence

Personal trainers can be tempted to practice outside of the scope of their certification, especially when clients ask for their advice on topics better suited to physical therapy or a rehabilitation specialist. It can also be tempting at the end of a long day for a personal trainer to become distracted and not pay attention to the client, which can increase the possibility of injury. Also, when the trainer and client become very familiar with each other, they may be more likely to chat freely during the session. This sometimes encourages the personal trainer to not pay attention to technique as diligently as he might otherwise have.

Risk management techniques to minimize liability

Personal trainers must take care to keep their eyes and ears open at all times for the safety of their clients. Cell phones and anything else that would be distracting to the trainer should be put away. Sessions should be properly documented so if any questions arise, they can be answered in a timely way. Where necessary, the trainer should keep medical personnel up-to-date with pertinent information regarding the client. Clients should not be allowed to exercise on equipment that exceeds their current abilities, and trainers should not promise to help with training details that lie outside their scope of practice.

Equipment maintenance and client safety

Equipment should be checked weekly to ensure it remains in proper working order. If it isn't working properly, a sign should be put in clear view that puts the machine out of commission until maintenance is able to fix the issue. If equipment is broken, the client may be injured while trying to operate it.

Modeling positive behaviors

One of the most important things the trainer can do for the client is to model positive behaviors. For instance, a courteous tone of voice when addressing the client, professional dress, actively listening to client issues, and not smoking are positive behaviors to demonstrate for the client. Additionally, it is best when the trainer models the behaviors that he expects from his clients; for instance, being early to appointments, eating with proper nutrition, and exercising consistently during the week. The trainer should have a "do as I do" attitude towards the client.

Manipulating exercise environment to provide a positive experience

If the client is anxious about working out at a public fitness facility, the personal trainer can do a variety of things to ensure the client is comfortable. The trainer should start with machines that the client is a little more familiar and comfortable with before introducing foreign ones. The trainer should be early so she can greet the client, never making the client have to search for her to begin the session. If crowds make the client uncomfortable, the personal trainer can try to meet with the client during a time of day when the facility may be less crowded. The trainer should make sure the client knows where everything is located inside the facility and ensure he has all the tools he needs to be able to exercise alone.

Limiting distractions during training sessions

Personal trainers can limit distractions during a training session simply by putting their phone away and not having conversations with others who happen to pass by. Additionally, trainers can limit conversation with clients during the session to what pertains to the exercise routine itself. Personal conversations can occur prior to or after the session. Clients should feel that all attention is on them for the duration of the session and that their money is going to a productive exercise session. Avoiding distractions makes the session safer and more enjoyable for the client.

Safeguarding personal intellectual property

The personal trainer should copyright material that is his personal intellectual property. In order to do this, the trainer needs to be familiar with national and international copyright laws and access the proper avenues to copyright material. Anything original to the personal trainer may be copyrighted and safeguarded in his name.

Documentation of work not original to the personal trainer

Material that is not original to the personal trainer should be documented and cited whenever it is used. Trainers need to be aware that even though information may be well known publicly, it must still be cited when used on blogs, websites, or printed materials. At a minimum, the title of the resource, name of the author, when the resource was published, and where it can be found should be included in the citation.

Developing original educational materials

It is for the personal trainer's benefit to have educational materials ready for clients prior to actually needing them. When a trainer first starts sessions with a client, she should ask the client what he would like to be educated on and perhaps give him a variety of topics to choose from. Materials should be formatted so they are concise and easy to understand. All educational material should be properly cited unless the information is unique to the personal trainer. Having personal, original educational material is valuable for a trainer to have as part of her portfolio. Additionally, as the portfolio grows, it will benefit clients because there will be a wide array of educational topics for them to choose from.

Privacy and confidentiality for clients

The personal trainer can easily ensure privacy and confidentiality for a client by ensuring all computer files are password protected and information is shared only with those for whom the client has given permission. Information should optimally be shared over the phone or in person rather than email, or ideally, emails should be encrypted if they must be used. The rule of thumb is to make sure the client gives permission for passing on personal information.

Client privacy means that individual client information is privy only to the client it pertains to, and possibly to medical personnel. In some cases, the client may give permission for information to be shared with certain family members, but that permission should be obtained in writing from the client. Personal client information should never be shared over social media or with other trainers.

FERPA and HIPAA laws

The FERPA (Family Educational Rights and Privacy Act) and HIPAA (Health Insurance Portability and Accountability Act) laws protect the privacy of the individual. In personal training, the trainer should only share what is minimally necessary for the benefit of the client and only where permission has been obtained. Client information should also be stored in a safe place that doesn't have public access, preferably under lock and key.

The personal trainer should follow FERPA and HIPAA guidelines where appropriate for his practice. Since health information is private and confidential, the trainer needs to take every precaution to ensure it is not accidentally shared with inappropriate outside sources. The trainer needs to make a practice of filing and locking client information and keeping it in his office rather than taking it to his place of residence.

Client health and contact information

Prior to a training session, the personal trainer should always have the client's file where emergency contact information can be easily found. The trainer should never begin a training session without having that client's file. The file can include session notes and previous workout sessions. This way, if the client has questions about her progress, the information is easily accessible in the moment.

Practice Test

1. The joint movement that results in an increase of the joint angle is called
    a. Abduction
    b. Adduction
    c. Extension
    d. Flexion

2. Which of these muscles is not part of the Rotator cuff?
    a. Supraspinatus
    b. Infraspinatus
    c. Teres minor
    d. Teres major

3. Which of the following should be considered a life-threatening medical emergency?
    a. Anterior cruciate ligament tear
    b. A dislocation of the cervical spinal cord
    c. An Achilles' tendon rupture
    d. A hip fracture in an elderly individual

4. Which of the following can cause pain in the lumbar area?
    a. Strain of the tibialis anterior muscle
    b. Strain of the longissimus thoracis muscle
    c. Strain of the gastrocnemius muscle
    d. Strain of the sternocleidomastoid muscle

5. When working with a trainer, an individual lifts a 10-pound weight straight over her head through a distance of 2.5 feet. How much linear work has been generated?
    a. 4 pound-feet
    b. 7.5 pound-feet
    c. 25 pound-feet
    d. 50 pound-feet

6. For average groups of people represented below, which order represents the lowest resting heart rate to the highest resting heart rate?
    a. Men, women, children, elderly individuals
    b. Children, women, elderly individuals, men
    c. Elderly individuals, women, men, children
    d. Elderly individuals, men, women, children

7. The body recruits type I muscle fibers for activities of
    a. long duration and low intensity
    b. long duration and high intensity
    c. short duration and high intensity
    d. none of the above

8. All of the following classes of nutrients provide sources of energy EXCEPT
    a. proteins
    b. vitamins
    c. fats
    d. carbohydrates

9. A nonathlete who weighs 80 kg would require _____ grams per day of protein.
   a. 50 grams
   b. 80 grams
   c. 64 grams
   d. 100 grams

10. A deficiency of which vitamin can lead to difficulty seeing at night and an increased susceptibility to infections?
    a. vitamin B1
    b. vitamin B3
    c. vitamin E
    d. vitamin A

11. You are exercising outdoors and become concerned that your client may be dehydrated. At what point would her condition be considered a medical emergency?
    a. When she complains that her leg muscles are cramping
    b. When she seems to be confused and doesn't know where she is
    c. When she becomes dizzy and light-headed
    d. When she begins complaining of a headache

12. What food information is NOT present on a food label?
    a. amount of protein in a serving
    b. amount of cholesterol in a serving
    c. amount of calories in a serving
    d. amount of caffeine in a serving

13. When meeting with a client for the first time, all of the following can be helpful comments to make to a client EXCEPT
    a. "How would you like this work to help you?"
    b. "Can you tell me about your daily routine?"
    c. "What heath problems do you have?"
    d. "Do you think you have clinical depression?"

14. A client in the precontemplation stage of behavior might think to himself:
    a. "I just can't lose weight."
    b. "I have a plan to lose weight."
    c. "I am really thinking about how to lose weight."
    d. "I am so proud I lost weight!"

15. An example of a substitution behavioral change that you might suggest to a client is
    a. "Call your best friend to walk with you every day."
    b. "Take the stairs instead of the elevator at work."
    c. "If you reach this goal we set up, you can have a reward of your choosing."
    d. "Put your running shoes right by your bed so you are motivated to run first thing in the morning."

16. Your client is in the maintenance stage of behavior and is exercising regularly. One day she cancels her appointments with you, claiming she has too much to do at work. If she abandons her exercise routine completely, it is called a
    a. lapse
    b. self-change
    c. relapse
    d. self-challenge

17. All of the following can help the client-trainer relationship EXCEPT
    a. Accepting your client for what she is able to do, even if others her age are able to do more
    b. Asking your client about his week
    c. Answering a text or phone call during a session
    d. Keeping information between the two of you confidential

18. An example of active listening is
    a. "Why didn't you do this exercise this week?"
    b. "Great job with your exercises this week!"
    c. "How did your big project at work turn out?"
    d. "So you are saying that you didn't understand how this exercise was supposed to feel?"

19. The interactive tool that can lead to change by creating an equal partnership between the client and the trainer is called
    a. Motivational interviewing
    b. Generative moments
    c. Appreciative inquiry
    d. Change talk

20. Goals that a trainer helps a client set should be all of the following EXCEPT
    a. Time-limited
    b. Action-based
    c. Broadly defined
    d. Measurable

21. Active listening, building rapport, and showing understanding of a client's situation are all components of
    a. Nonverbal communication
    b. Intrinsic motivation
    c. Extrinsic motivation
    d. Client-centered techniques

22. As a prelude to creating a personal training package for a client, a trainer should obtain all of the following EXCEPT
    a. Approval and signature of a physician
    b. Informed consent from the client
    c. Permission to post the client's photo on the trainer's Web site
    d. Health history of the client

23. A number of atherosclerotic cardiovascular disease risk factors exist. A client who has which of the following would be considered to have a positive risk factor for hypertension?
    a. Systolic blood pressure $\geq$ 140 mm Hg on two separate occasions
    b. Diastolic blood pressure $\geq$75 mm Hg on two separate occasions
    c. Systolic blood pressure $\geq$ 140 mm Hg and diastolic blood pressure $\geq$ 100 mm Hg on one occasion
    d. Having taken an antihypertensive medication in the past

24. Shortness of breath at rest is called
    a. Ischemia
    b. Dyspnea
    c. Syncope
    d. Orthopnea

25. All of the following are true of intermittent claudication EXCEPT
    a. People with diabetes have a greater risk of having intermittent claudication.
    b. Intermittent claudication does not usually occur when a client stands or sits.
    c. Intermittent claudication usually goes away within 10 minutes of stopping an exercise.
    d. Symptoms associated with intermittent claudication are reproducible.

26. Which of the following pulses is not commonly used to determine an individual's heart rate?
    a. Carotid
    b. Brachial
    c. Radial
    d. Popliteal

27. Normal systolic and diastolic blood pressure measurements (in mm Hg) include which of the following?
    a. Systolic 110, diastolic 75
    b. Systolic 130, diastolic 70
    c. Systolic 140, diastolic 85
    d. Systolic 110, diastolic 85

28. An individual weighs 80 kg and is 1.73 meters tall. What range does his BMI fall into?
    a. Normal
    b. Overweight
    c. Obese class I
    d. Obese class II

29. The Rockport is a field test that involves
    a. Running continuously for 1.5 miles
    b. Walking intermittently for 2 miles
    c. Stepping up and down continuously for 3 minutes
    d. Walking as fast as possible for 1 mile

30. An individual's flexibility can be assessed by which of the following?
    a. A one-repetition bench press
    b. A sit-and-reach test
    c. A push-up test
    d. A curl-up test

31. The hip joint is what type of joint?
    a. Ball-and-socket joint
    b. Hinge joint
    c. Cartilaginous joint
    d. Pivot joint

32. The primary function of the respiratory system is
    a. Delivering nutrients to tissues in the body
    b. Regulating the body's pH level
    c. Facilitating the exchange of oxygen and carbon dioxide
    d. Maintaining fluid volume to prevent dehydration

33. The type of stretching that requires assistance from a personal trainer is called
    a. Active stretching
    b. Passive stretching
    c. Ballistic stretching
    d. Static stretching

34. All of the following are benefits of increased flexibility EXCEPT
    a. Improved circulation
    b. Increased range of motion
    c. Improved coordination
    d. Increased chance of muscle injury

35. The condition that involves rapid breakdown of muscle tissue due to too much exercise, which can potentially result in kidney failure, is called
    a. Myoglobinuria
    b. Rhabdomyolysis
    c. Dialysis
    d. Proteinuria

36. Benefits of nonlinear periodized training programs include all of the following EXCEPT
    a. Using a progressive increase in the workout intensity
    b. Allowing for variation in the workout intensity
    c. Having a "power" training day
    d. Training both power and strength of muscles within one week

37. What is the approximate target heart rate for a 50-year-old man in beats per minute (bpm)?
    a. 75 to 120
    b. 85 to 110
    c. 85 to 145
    d. 120 to 160

38. An effective cardiorespiratory training program session should include all of these basic components EXCEPT
    a. Power phase
    b. Cool-down phase
    c. Warm-up phase
    d. Endurance phase

39. The "talk test" refers to
    a. The practice of speaking with your client before a training session to check in with the client
    b. The practice of talking with your client during the cool-down phase to see how the session felt.
    c. The ability of an individual while exercising to talk or respond to a trainer's questions without gasping for breath.
    d. The comfort level of a client to let a trainer know when an exercise is too hard.

40. Individuals with osteoporosis
    a. Should not do flexibility training exercises
    b. Should avoid twisting or flexing of the spine
    c. Should not worry about proper breathing techniques
    d. Are not more likely to develop fractures

41. Which of the following inhibits a person's joint flexibility?
    a. Having cold muscles
    b. Being a woman
    c. Having more relaxed muscles
    d. Having a more physically active lifestyle

42. Older adults should engage in an aerobic exercise program that provides which of the following?
    a. 25 minutes, 3 days a week of mild intensity aerobic activity
    b. 30 minutes, 3 days a week of moderate intensity aerobic activity
    c. 20 minutes, 5 days a week of vigorous intensity aerobic activity
    d. 30 minutes, 5 days a week of moderate intensity aerobic activity

43. Which of the following conditions is an absolute contraindication for exercising during pregnancy?
    a. Poorly controlled seizure disorder
    b. Ruptured membranes
    c. Heavy smoker
    d. Poorly controlled hypertension

44. Common complications of diabetes include all of the following EXCEPT
    a. Kidney problems
    b. Vision problems
    c. Hearing problems
    d. Peripheral nerve problems

45. How much weight loss is appropriate for an obese individual with a BMI greater than 30?
    a. 1 kg a week
    b. 2 kg a week
    c. 3 kg a week
    d. 4 kg a week

46. Which of the following is not covered when obtaining informed consent from a client?
    a. Benefits that the client should expect to gain
    b. Risks and discomfort that may be associated with the training program
    c. Purpose of the training program
    d. How much the training program will cost

47. The end of a bone is called the
    a. Epiphysis
    b. Periosteum
    c. Endosteum
    d. Diaphysis

48. All are true of a synovial joint EXCEPT
    a. The synovial cavity is filled with synovial fluid.
    b. A synovial joint can flex and extend.
    c. A synovial joint may be supported by ligaments.
    d. A synovial joint never contains any other structures inside of it.

49. Leg raises are an example of
    a. Hip extension
    b. Knee flexion
    c. Hip flexion
    d. Hip abduction

50. Which function does the autonomic nervous system NOT regulate?
    a. Digestion
    b. Breathing
    c. Running
    d. Secretion of hormones

Answers and Explanations

1. C: When a joint is extended, the angle of the joint is increased. Flexion is the opposite of extension, and causes the joint angle to decrease. Abduction refers to movement that is directed away from the midline of the body. The opposite of abduction is adduction. Adduction describes movements that are made toward the midline of the body.

2. D: The Supraspinatus is an abductor of the arm. The Infraspinatus and Teres minor are both external rotators. The Subscapularis is the missing muscle of the rotator cuff.

3. B: Any trauma to the neck (or cervical spine) should be considered a medical emergency. When the cervical vertebrae are dislocated or fractured, the spinal column can become unstable. This can potentially lead to paralysis or death. While an Achilles' tendon rupture or anterior cruciate ligament tear is a serious leg/knee injury, respectively, and may be career ending for athletes, either one is not life threatening. A hip fracture or a fracture of the neck of the femur can cause permanent disability, especially in the elderly. However, these are also not usually life threatening.

4. B: The longissimus thoracis muscle is located in the posterior lumbar region. It is part of the erector spinae group. These muscles help maintain posture and provide stability to the spine. Lumbar pain, also called low back pain, is one of the most common causes of disability. About 60 to 80% of the general population will experience it at some point in their lives. Determining the specific cause of lumbar pain may be difficult, but muscle strain, an intervertebral herniated disc, and joint inflammation can all cause lumbar pain. The other muscles are not located in the lumbar region. The sternocleidomastoid muscle is located in the cervical region. Strain to this muscle occurs with "whiplash" injuries. The tibialis anterior muscle is located on the anterior and lateral part of the lower leg. The gastrocnemius muscle is located on the posterior part of the lower leg.

5. C: Multiplying the force times the distance through which the force travels will result in the linear work generated. Ten times 2.5 equals 25.

6. D: Heart rate is the number of times that the heart beats per minute and can be measured by taking a pulse. Average people have a resting heart rate of 60 to 80 beats per minute (bpm). The elderly have a lower resting heart rate than adult men and women. Men have a resting heart rate that is about 10 bpm lower than that of adult women. Children have resting heart rates that are higher than those of adults. When comparing fit to unfit individuals, fit individuals have a lower resting heart rate.

7. A: The body has two types of muscle fibers: type I and type II. Together, these muscle fibers can do all types of tasks. However, the body recruits each type during different activities or specific times of an activity, depending on the type and duration of motion required. Type I muscle fibers, also called slow-twitch fibers, are used for activities of long duration and low intensity, such as those involving endurance. In contrast, type II muscle fibers are employed for high-speed, high-power tasks. These muscle fibers are capable of generating force more quickly than type I muscle fibers.

8. B: Carbon is critical for the energy production process. Proteins, fats, and carbohydrates—which are all sources of carbon—contribute to a number of functions in the body. They help provide energy so that muscles, nerves, and metabolic processes work normally. Energy is measured in calories (cal) or kilocalories (kcal). When individuals exercise, they can "burn" energy more quickly. Vitamins and minerals are critical for providing essential nutrients that the body needs to maintain normal function; however, they are not a source of energy.

9. C: The average person's daily requirement for protein is 0.8 g/kg. In other words, multiplying 0.8 by the person's weight in kilograms will give the daily amount of protein in grams needed. For this individual, that would be $80 \times 0.8 = 64$ grams. Athletes require more protein each day—about 1.2 to 2 g/kg of body weight. If this individual were an athlete, he or she would require between 96 and 160 grams of protein per day. In addition to these specific recommendations, it is also recommended that protein account for about 12 to 15% of the total calories a person eats each day.

10. D: Vitamin A, known as retinol, is found in foods such as fish liver oils, butter, and egg yolks. It is critical for red blood cell and embryo development and normal functioning of the eyes, the immune system, and the skin. Vitamin B_1 is also called thiamin. A deficiency of this vitamin can lead to beriberi. Symptoms of beriberi can include cardiovascular problems, peripheral neuropathy, and cognitive and psychiatric problems. Vitamin B_3 is also known as niacin; a deficiency of this vitamin can cause a disease called pellagra. Pellagra can cause a skin rash, gastrointestinal symptoms, or cognitive difficulties. If untreated, it can also lead to death. Vitamin E is an antioxidant that augments the immune system. It can help prevent cell membranes from being destroyed by harmful free radicals.

11. B: Dehydration, heat exhaustion, and heat stroke are conditions that are best avoided by encouraging clients to drink either water or sports drinks often. When individuals wait until they feel thirsty to drink, they may already have lost 1 to 2 liters of fluid. A dehydrated individual may feel less energetic and begin to develop muscle cramps. If not treated, an individual can develop heat exhaustion, which may be manifested by headaches and feelings of nausea. If heat exhaustion isn't treated, an individual may suffer from heat stroke. During heat stroke, an individual's body temperature increases, and he or she may become confused or lose consciousness. This is a medical emergency. The patient needs to have her body temperature lowered as quickly as possible.

12. D: Labeling on food packages is helpful in determining a number of characteristics of a food, including the ingredients, serving size, and nutrients present in the food. Food label information is based on a 2,000 calorie diet. It provides the percent daily value for the amount of fats, cholesterol, sodium, potassium, carbohydrates, and protein present in a serving size. While caffeine will be listed as an ingredient if it is present in the food, the specific amount of caffeine will not be listed.

13. D: It is important to remember that coaching is not therapy or mental health counseling. Personal trainers should never diagnose current psychiatric problems. However, it is important to ask a person about their past history—medical and otherwise—so that your sessions can be appropriate and productive. Knowing about a person's daily routine will tell you how active he or she usually is. Asking, "How would you like this work to help you?" can elicit a specific goal that the two of you can work toward.

14. A: There are five stages of behavioral change. Listed in order of unwilling to change to readiness to change, they are precontemplation, contemplation, preparation, action, and maintenance. People in precontemplation often say, "I can't" or "I won't" about being able to change. People in the contemplation stage often say, "I just may change" or "I'm thinking about it." People in the preparation stage have actively decided to take action at some point soon. In the action stage, a person has decided to implement a consistent change, but has been implementing the new behavior for less than six months. If a person has consistently implemented a change for more than six months, he or she is in the maintenance stage.

15. B: There are a number of strategies trainers can employ in order to effect behavior change in a client. Substitution or counterconditioning involves substituting healthy behaviors for unhealthy behaviors. Answer A is an example of social support. Answer C is an example of a reward or reinforcement system. Answer D is an example of environmental control, which is a cue that can precipitate healthy behavior.

16. C: A relapse is when a person stops their positive behavior and, as a result, loses the positive benefits he or she had gained. Many conditions can lead to relapse; work pressures, boredom, and increased travel are only a few. Although similar, a lapse is a temporary stop in positive behavior. Had this client returned after a week or two, her exercise routine would have lapsed, but she would have likely maintained or quickly regained the positive benefits.

17. C: A number of factors can help facilitate a beneficial working relationship between a client and a trainer. These can include being present in the moment, maintaining confidentiality, being interested in your client's life, giving helpful feedback, and treating your client in a positive way. Along those lines, it is important to accept clients at the level they are currently at, rather than comparing them to others.

18. D: Active listening is a technique than enhances communication. It involves conveying what the client says back to the client, so that the individual feels they are being heard and understood. The client tells you how he or she feels or what he or she thinks, and you repeat or paraphrase it back to the individual. This technique provides the opportunity for clarification in the event that the client actually meant something else. When actively listening, it is helpful to let the other speak without interruption and to maintain eye contact and focus on the client.

19. A: Motivational interviewing is based on the idea that change occurs when there is an equal partnership between the client and trainer. While you are a training expert, your client is an expert is his or her own life. Motivational interviewing is used in a client-centered relationship. Generative moments are powerful or negative events that have happened to a client that can spur him or her to change. Appreciative inquiry is a technique in which the trainer asks positive and powerful questions to help the client visualize potential possibilities. Change talk involves language spoken by a client about his or her desire and ability to change their behavior.

20. C: Goals that are most helpful are those that are specific, very well defined, able to be measured, realistic, and have a time constraint on them. The actions a client needs to take should be specifically defined. For example, a goal may be that a client will walk on his treadmill at a pace of 3 mph for 30 minutes on Monday through Friday before going to work.

21. D: Client-centered techniques include asking open-ended questions, listening actively, and frequently clarifying what the client says. These can all contribute to building rapport and a strong relationship with a client. Nonverbal communication is that which is expressed and received via nonverbal cues, such as facial expressions, gestures, and the presence or absence of eye contact. Intrinsic motivation is the motivation for change that comes from within. For example, a person may want to lose weight to feel proud or to feel like he can achieve a goal. When people are extrinsically motivated, they are motivated to achieve a goal because of an external factor. For example, someone might want to lose weight to fit into a wedding dress.

22. C: While you should always obtain permission before posting a photo of a client on a Web site, that is not one of the critical initial pieces of information. If medical clearance is necessary, a signature and recommendations from your client's physician should be obtained. In addition, you will need to know your client's past and present medical and health issues to create an appropriate training plan. You will also need informed consent from your client, demonstrating that he or she understands the risk and benefits of undertaking a training program.

23. A: Hypertension is defined by the Seventh Report of the Joint National Committee on Prevention, Detection, Evaluation, and Treatment of High Blood Pressure as a systolic blood pressure of $\geq$ 140 mm Hg and a diastolic blood pressure of $\geq$ 90 mm Hg on two separate occasions. In addition, current use of an antihypertensive medication is considered to be a positive risk factor for hypertension.

24. B: A client with dyspnea will have shortness of breath while resting or only with mild exertion. It is not normal, and it can be a symptom of cardiac or pulmonary disease. Orthopnea is shortness of breath that occurs when one is lying down. It is relieved by sitting upright or standing. Ischemia occurs when there is a lack of blood flow and oxygen to the heart. This causes pain in the chest or pain that has radiated to the neck or arm. Syncope is a loss of consciousness that usually occurs when the brain does not receive enough oxygen.

25. C: When an individual has intermittent claudication, he or she will develop pain in a specific area with exercise due to inadequate blood flow to that specific muscle. This pain can be reproduced from day to day. It usually does not occur when a client is sitting or standing. People with coronary artery disease or diabetes are prone to developing intermittent claudication. However, once the exercise that precipitated the pain has stopped, the pain should go away within one to two minutes.

26. D: The popliteal artery, located behind the knee, can be difficult to palpate. The carotid pulse is felt by placing one's fingers lightly in the lower neck, along the medial aspect of the sternocleidomastoid muscle. The brachial pulse can be palpated between the triceps and biceps muscles on the anterior and medial aspect of the arm, near the elbow. The radial artery can be palpated on the anterior arm, near the wrist.

27. A: Normal blood pressure is classified as a systolic pressure of less than 120 mm Hg and a diastolic pressure of less than 80 mm Hg. If either the systolic or diastolic pressures are elevated on multiple occasions, an individual's blood pressure is considered to be high.

28. B: BMI stands for body mass index, and it can be calculated by dividing an individual's weight by height squared. In this example, BMI = 80 kg / $(1.73 \text{ m})^2$. This results is a BMI of 26.7. BMI values fall into a range. The normal range is 18.5–24.9. The overweight range is 25–29.9. The obese class I range is 30–34.9. The obese class II range is 35–39.9.

29. D: The Rockport 1-mile walk test involves having a client walk as fast as he or she can for a distance of 1 mile. The individual must not run at all during this test. At the end of the test, the individual's pulse and heart rate are measured. The Queens College Step Test involves having an individual step up and down on a standardized step height continuously for 3 minutes and then measuring his or her pulse and heart rate after the 3 minutes.

30. B: A sit-and-reach test can measure the flexibility of an individual's lower back, hip, and hamstrings. A one-repetition bench press is used to assess muscular strength or muscle force. Both the push-up test and the curl-up test are used for measuring muscle endurance.

31. A: The hip joint as well as the shoulder joint can move in all directions. They are ball-and-socket joints. A hinge joint can only move in one plane, such as with knee flexion and extension. A cartilaginous joint is a strong joint that is very slightly movable, such as intervertebral joints. A pivot joint is a joint in one plane that permits rotation, such as the humeroradial joint.

32. C: The respiratory system involves the lungs and is where the exchange of oxygen for carbon dioxide occurs. The cardiovascular system, which involves the heart and blood vessels, is responsible for delivering oxygen and nutrients to all tissues in the body, regulating the body's pH level to prevent acidosis or alkalosis, and maintaining fluid volume to prevent dehydration.

33. B: In passive stretching, a client remains relaxed, allowing a trainer to stretch the client's muscles. Ballistic stretching, which involves a bouncing-like movement, can cause injury to muscles if not performed carefully. Static stretching involves movements that are deliberate and sustained. Active stretching involves stretching muscles throughout their range of motion.

34. D: Flexibility training has a number of benefits, including increased circulation, increased range of motion, improved muscle coordination, and decreased future chance of muscle injury.

35. B: Rhabdomyolysis, caused when an individual exercises too excessively, results in muscle damage and breakdown. These breakdown products, which can include protein and myoglobin, then enter the bloodstream and have the potential to harm the kidneys. Kidney failure, and possibly death, can result. Symptoms of rhabdomyolysis can include muscle swelling, pain, and soreness. Myoglobinuria and proteinuria describe the conditions of having myoglobin and protein in the urine. However, they do necessarily reflect a cause. Dialysis is a treatment for kidney failure.

36. A: While a linear periodized training program involves having a progressive increase in the workout intensity over the course of a week, a nonlinear periodized training program involves variation of intensity over the course of a week. A weeklong nonlinear periodized training program can target both muscle strength and power. A "power" training day involving power sets can also be implemented. This type of program may be more conducive to individuals with scheduling conflicts.

37. C: To calculate an individual's target heart rate, first one needs to estimate the person's maximal heart rate. This is estimated by subtracting a person's age from 220. In this example, the person's maximal heart rate is 220– 50 = 170. Using this number, the target heart rate can be calculated. The recommended target heart rate is between 50% and 85% of the maximal heart rate. This would be 170 × 0.50 = 85, and 170 × 0.85 = 145. So, the individual's target heart rate is estimated to be between about 85 and 145 bpm.

38. A: A training program needs to balance many different variables in order to be effective. A trainer needs to take a client's goals, daily routines, and preferences into account to create a routine that will be followed. Each training session should include a warm-up phase, a workout or endurance phase, and then a cool-down phase.

39. C: It is important that a training session not be too intense. The "talk test" is a simple way to get a handle on the intensity of the endurance or workout phase. A client should be able to talk or answer a trainer's questions without gasping for breath. Not being able to speak easily can indicate that the workout is too intense. Cardiovascular, muscular, and orthopedic injuries are more likely to occur when a workout is too intense.

40. B: Osteoporosis is a disease that involves a loss of bone mineral density. Osteopenia is a milder form of osteoporosis. Although people with osteoporosis are more susceptible to fractures due to the thinning of their bones, they are appropriate candidates for flexibility training programs. These programs can help improve posture and maintain the alignment of the spine. However, the program should avoid repetitive exercises that involve twisting or flexing of the spine. Everyone who participates in a flexibility training program should be taught proper breathing techniques.

41. A: A person's flexibility is reflected in his or her ability to move a joint, without pain, through a range of motion. In general, a number of factors are associated with increased flexibility. Younger people are more flexible than older individuals, and women are more flexible than men. Warmer, more relaxed muscles allow more joint flexibility than colder muscles. Individuals who are physically active are often more flexible than those who are not. In addition, the joint structure and health of the joint and its surrounding tissues affect an individual's flexibility.

42. D: If their medical issues allow it, individuals over the age of 65 can and should participate in exercise training programs. Aerobic, or cardiorespiratory, exercise can decrease morbidity and mortality rates in older individuals. The recommendations are for older individuals to engage in moderate intensity aerobic activity for 30 minutes, 5 days a week (150 minutes total), or to engage in vigorous intensity aerobic activity for 25 minutes, 3 days a week (75 minutes total). People can also do a combination of both.

43. B: Recent research supports a role for exercise programs during pregnancy. Goals of this type of program can include reducing low back pain and decreasing the risk for developing gestational diabetes. However, there do exist a number of absolute contraindications. Some of these include ruptured membranes, placenta previa after 26 weeks of gestation, premature labor, preeclampsia, and high-risk multiple gestation pregnancies. In contrast, relative contraindications include the individual being a heavy smoker, having poorly controlled diabetes or seizures, or having poorly controlled hypertension or hyperthyroid disease.

44. C: Diabetes can lead to kidney problems (nephropathy), trouble seeing (retinopathy), and decreased sensation of peripheral nerves (peripheral neuropathy). If these conditions are present, a trainer needs to adapt an exercise program accordingly. Some precautions that can be taken include keeping the blood pressure stable for retinopathy, avoiding exercise requiring high levels of coordination for peripheral neuropathy, or avoiding prolonged exercise for nephropathy.

45. A: People who are obese have a BMI greater than or equal to 30. These individuals are at a high risk of cardiac problems, certain types of cancers, and diabetes. Among other areas, training programs can focus on weight loss, promoting appetite control, and lowering the risk of associated medical issues. Weight loss should be gradual—not more than 1 kg per week. Aerobic training sessions five to seven times a week lasting 45–60 minutes per session may be helpful.

46. D: Obtaining informed consent at the beginning of a professional relationship can protect against potential later legal action. An informed consent document will discuss the reason for the training program, the risks or discomfort that a client may experience, the responsibilities of the client, the benefits the client may reap, and it will offer the opportunity for a client to ask related questions. Fee structure and payments are not part of the informed consent.

47. A: When describing the anatomy of a bone, the epiphysis is the end of a bone and the diaphysis is the shaft of the bone. The periosteum is a membrane that covers the surface of a bone, except at the articular surfaces (joints). The endosteum is the lining of the bone marrow cavity and contains the cells necessary for new bone development.

48. D: A synovial joint is the most common type of joint found in the body and is made up of two articulating bones. Synovial fluid is present in the synovial cavity, which is lined by a synovial membrane. The joint is surrounded by a fibrous capsule, which can be supported by ligaments. Sometimes, a synovial joint may contain other structures, such as menisci (for example, in the knee) or fat pads. There are subtypes of synovial joints, including a hinge joint, ball-and-socket joint, and a pivot joint.

49. C: Leg raises are one type of exercise that works the hip flexor muscles. These muscles include the iliopsoas, rectus femoris, sartorius, and pectineus. Exercises for hip extension include squats or leg presses. Hip extensor muscles are the hamstrings and the gluteus maximus. Hip abduction exercises can be done with an exercise machine. Muscles involved with hip abduction include the tensor fascia latae, sartorius, and gluteus minimus and medius. Leg curl exercises involve knee flexion. Muscles involved with flexion of the knee are the hamstrings, gracilis, and popliteus.

50. C: The central nervous system is comprised of the brain and the spinal cord and is responsible for receiving, analyzing, interpreting, and acting on sensory information. The central nervous system is comprised of the peripheral and autonomic nervous systems. The autonomic nervous system is responsible for functions such as respiration, digestion, making hormones, and maintaining heart rate. The autonomic nervous system can be subdivided into the sympathetic nervous system, which is activated when the body is "stressed" and causes an increase in heart rate and respiratory rate and the parasympathetic nervous system, which is "in control" when the stressful stimulus is no longer present.

36549391R00040

Made in the USA
San Bernardino, CA
26 July 2016